My Life Is Failure

Jim Johnson

The Standish Group International, Inc

Copyright © 2006

by

The Standish Group International, Incorporated

Published by:

The Standish Group International, Inc.
196 Old Townhouse Road
West Yarmouth, MA 02673
508-760-3600
www.standishgroup.com

This book is based on the CHAOS Chronicles Version 5.0.7

ISBN 1-4243-0841-0

Printed in the United States of America

To my wife and life-long companion, Nancy

Acknowledgement

This book was not written by me. I was merely the instrument of compilation and synthesis of the hearts and minds of the thousands of contributors. In that regard, my deep appreciation to Karen Larkowski, who is the force behind CHAOS University and the CHAOS Chronicles. Thanks to Jim Crear who kept me on the straight and narrow on so many issues and Sidnie Feit for her help in the understanding of the numbers and her efforts on the workshops and focus groups.

Recognition goes to Gordon Divitt for his forthright and incisive critiques on the early drafts. To Ed Schaider for his unique perspective and insight on all things chaotic. To Colleen Fry whose patience in editing is commendable. To Robbie Sibley, who not only edited many versions, but also took great care of the delegates to CHAOS University. To my sister, Bonnie, on her editing and helpful perceptive.

Credit to Mike Deutsch for his fine art work. To Chuck Saling on the development of the online surveys and the knowledge center. Thanks to all the Standish members who helped along the way. Thanks to the thousands of SURF members and CHAOS University attendees whose contribution made this work possible.

Introduction

The Sydney Opera House in Australia is a national symbol. It is one of the truly great icons of the world and the most widely known opera house in the universe.

It is also the home of the greatest project management failure in the history of mankind. It has the smallest opera stage in the world and is void of truly great performances. Its operational labor cost per seat is twice that of other opera houses. It is a marvel to behold, an enigma to be pondered.

The Sydney Opera House is a classic project management failure. First, it had a revolutionary design, but many of the construction concepts were not tested. Second, there were many "ready-fire-aim" situations; a prime example is that the foundation was built while the upper structure was still in design. Third, user input was disregarded. And the most damaging issue just might have been poor communication. Project leaders only communicated with sponsor representatives on a part-time basis, and when these sponsor representatives were replaced, as most of them frequently were, the new representatives stepped in with no detailed knowledge of current and past project events. The project's designers were also located more than 2,000 miles from the construction site. At one of the project's most crucial points, the two designers—the Danish Utzon and the English Arup—would not talk to each other, yet they were only separated by the North Sea.

My life is failure. I research failure, I write about failure, I breathe failure, and I owe my success to failure. My company, The Standish Group, has been collecting case information on real-life IT environments and software development projects since 1985. Standish Group's cumulative research encompasses 12 years of data on why projects succeed or fail, representing more than 50,000 completed IT projects. Through Standish Group's CHAOS University, we have hosted almost 500 workshops, as well as focus groups, project "group therapy" sessions, and executive retreats that focus on particular issues of project management. Our mission is to make you, the IT professional, more successful, and help show the value of your IT investments.

Chart 1

Project Resolution 2004

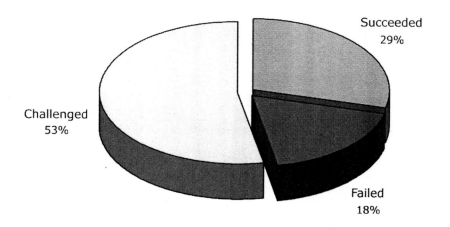

Source: CHAOS Database survey results, 2004

My friend, Jim Crear, a former CIO and highly experienced IT professional often says that complexity causes confusion, which ultimately leads to failure. So given his counsel, I have made this book simple, with 10 simple lessons covering the 10 CHAOS Success Factors: user involvement, executive support, clear business objectives, scope optimization, agile processes, project management expertise, financial management, skilled resources, formal methodology, and tools.

Gordon Divitt, a fairly salty Scotsman, a frequent delegate at CHAOS University, and another highly experienced IT professional, often questions the point of any discussion. Therefore, each lesson has 10 simple points. The lessons learned and their pertinent points derive from Standish Group's body of research on how to improve project success rates and reduce failures. Most of the quotes in the book are from presentations, workshops, and conversations at one of the many CHAOS University events. In most cases the quotes are from IT executives, such as chief information officers, chief technology officers, vice presidents of IS or other IT executive positions. Unless otherwise noted, the titles of individuals quoted herein will be from the above list.

These lessons are given as my opinions, but they are much more. They represent the accumulated knowledge of thousands of professionals about how you — the project manager, the application manager, the IT executive, or the business executive — should approach the development of application software.

Lack of user involvement is the number one reason for project failure. Conversely, it is also the number one contributor to project success. Even when delivered on time and on budget, a project can fail if it does not meet the users' needs or expectations, or if the user community does not accept the finished product.

Throughout the life of Standish Group's research efforts, much time has been spent trying to understand how to work better with the user community. "We don't exit the requirements phase until the client has signed off. Unless the customer says, 'That's what we want,' we do not execute — period," said Sanjiv Ahuja, past president of Telcordia Technologies (formerly Bellcore). Based on our research, our attempt was to understand what user facilities, procedures, characteristics, and skills could be brought to bear that would lead to project success.

Chart 2

Project Resolution by Type: 1994 - 2004

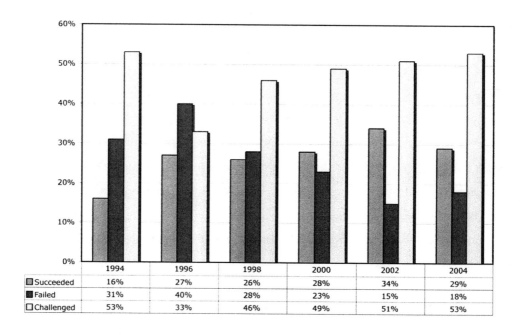

	1994	1996	1998	2000	2002	2004
Succeeded	16%	27%	26%	28%	34%	29%
Failed	31%	40%	28%	23%	15%	18%
Challenged	53%	33%	46%	49%	51%	53%

Source: CHAOS Database surveys results polled 1994 - 2004

Lesson One presents much of the research and thinking on this subject, condensed into these 10 points: Correctly identify the proper user. Develop and maintain a quality relationship with the user and user groups. Create and maintain a platform for communications in order to have a quality relationship with the users. Demonstrate results and understand why it is important to do so. Educate the users on the project management process and what their roles and responsibilities are within that process. Consider user feedback and consensus. Identify and recruit an evangelist. Show why and how to conduct primary research. Show respect for users. And focus, focus, focus on real user needs.

Every project has winners and losers. It is the business executives who ultimately determine whether or not a project will be a winner for the company. Many IT projects are the result of board-level decisions, and the fate of an executive is often riding on a successful outcome. During the years Standish Group has conducted research, the roles, responsibilities, and behavior of business executives have been of paramount interest.

Traditionally, executive support has occupied the number two spot in Standish's 10 CHAOS Success Factors. Our latest research confirms this is where it belongs; however, some people rank it even higher. "To us, having the support of executive management was much more important than having the users involved," said Isaac Applbaum, formerly of Bank of America. Executive management support influences the process and progress of a project. No matter what the case, it is fact that the lack of executive input and support can place a project at a severe disadvantage.

Lesson Two on executive support presents Standish's current thinking on this topic, condensed into these 10 points: Have a clear vision for the project that is easily understood. Get executive commitment. Make fast decisions. Have a decision pipeline. Focus on executive sponsor process education. Use measurements. Understand how and why you need to negotiate. Have a well-thought-out plan to convince the executive sponsor you are on target and gain his or her support. Understand the benefits of a kill switch and why every project should have one. Finally, appreciate the merits of celebration—and never take it lightly.

In addition to executive support, it is vital that every project have clear business objectives. Stakeholders measure projects based on factors such as customer satisfaction, increased revenue, or decreased cost.

All projects must have priorities based on business needs, whether they are short- or long-term goals. Some projects that may fall out of this category include those that repair broken systems, meet federal or other legislative mandates or rules, or are a general upgrade to the infrastructure. However, even these types of projects will only be judged successful if they meet some external benchmark.

Lesson Three on clear business objectives covers the following 10 points: Everyone involved must be on the same page in terms of the project's business objectives. Make sure stakeholders can recite the "elevator pitch," a concise and comprehensible explanation of the business objectives delivered in 10 seconds or less. Consider the big picture and how the project fits into the organization's overall strategy. Promote speed and understand how the clarity of business objectives can increase speed. Have a yardstick (project measurements). Make return on investment (ROI) a clear business objective. Collaborate with team members to ensure a clear and concise message on business objectives. Build the foundation for a peer review process. Avoid having too many cooks; too many stakeholders can spoil the project. Do your homework through basic and fundamental research and test the clarity and reliability of the business objectives.

The next factor for project success is scope optimization. My dog is a good illustration. The first time the veterinarian laid eyes on Manley he exclaimed, "He is nothing but a white ball of fur!" Manley, a Maltese, weighs only 10 pounds, but he lives up to his name. He is a fireball and will dominate dogs many times his size. He is optimal. He is small, but powerful, and that is how you want your software applications. You want them to be lean, mean, and powerful. You want them to be optimal. You want them to be like Manley. You do this by optimizing scope.

Chart 3

1994 - 2004 Average Percent Time Overruns

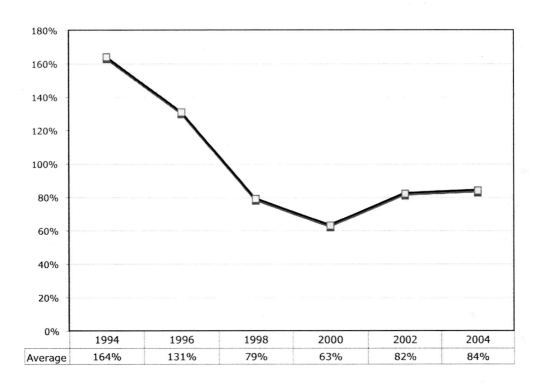

	1994	1996	1998	2000	2002	2004
Average	164%	131%	79%	63%	82%	84%

Source: CHAOS Database, surveys conducted 1994 thru 2004

Lesson Four on optimizing scope covers the following 10 points: Minimize scope to facilitate optimization. Understand the merits of stepping-stones and the dangers of milestones. Time is the enemy of all projects, so consider time boxing, which involves setting deadlines and a fixed amount of time in which to complete the project or stepping-stones. Examine the rules of engagement. Manage expectations by minimizing and optimizing the scope. Make use of a small medium, like an index card, to help optimize scope. Use role models as guides for both good and bad behavior. Assess the need of a requirement by its yield or gain. Consider the risk of each requirement. And finally, consider cost, risk, and gain as elements to optimizing scope. This point came out of an effort at a CHAOS University workshop to create a zoo, which is why it is named Panda Bear.

I cannot emphasize enough that time is the enemy of all projects and money is the root of all evil. When it comes to project success and features, you can never be too thin. You need to waste not, want not. Therefore, project teams should use an agile process, which is thin, with little waste. At the heart of all agile methods are an iterative development process and a design point that uses the bare minimum requirements. Through lessons learned from our collected CHAOS University experience, Standish Group continues to examine the reasons why project success can be achieved. There is no silver bullet, but agile methods come very close.

Lesson Five focuses on the agile methods and discusses the following 10 points: Use an iterative development style — it is the heart and soul of any agile process. Collaborate with team members as part of the agile development process. Follow up with rapid feedback, which promotes quickness and velocity — cornerstones of agile methods. Recognize that the agile process instills better testing and code quality controls than conventional software development. Consider the use of a Web-based standard infrastructure as a key component to the agile style. Ponder no new releases. This is one of our more controversial subjects, for it knocks down one of the software industry's biggest profit windmills. Organizations should go to a no-release policy and implement features and functions in a rapid pace on a standard infrastructure. More to come later!

Chart 4

1994 - 2004 Average Percent of Cost Overruns

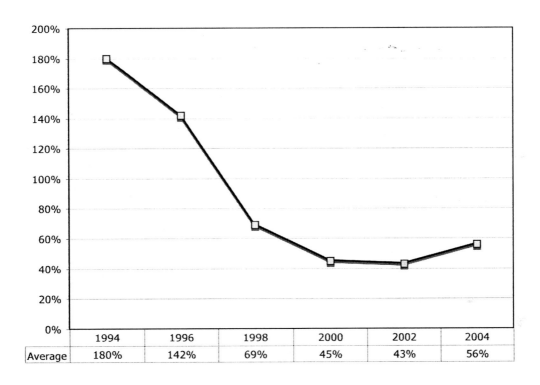

	1994	1996	1998	2000	2002	2004
Average	180%	142%	69%	45%	43%	56%

Source: CHAOS Database, surveys conducted 1994 thru 2004

The next two points describe the three most popular agile methodologies: Extreme Programming (XP), Rational Unified Process (RUP), and Scrum. And the last point includes this advice: Rethink that old adage about doing risky things first.

Even with an agile process, however, there is no substitute for the skills required to lead a project. Superman was faster than a speeding bullet. He was more powerful than a locomotive. He was able to leap tall buildings in a single bound. But let's face it: You are no Superman. You do not have x-ray vision, and it takes all your power to see through the lead wall of a project plan, never mind breaking through brick walls. Your powers are leadership and judgment.

Lesson Six covers project management expertise and the skills required to manage the projects, condensed into the following 10 points: Projects must follow project management fundamentals. Keep track of the all project management details—project managers need to plan for the changes or functions required to arrive at a goal. Project leaders should possess basic project management skills. Project managers need leadership qualities to be effective leaders. Make and maintain connections, as they are important to the success of a project. Promote both an individual and collective sense of ownership among the team — the sense of pride and accomplishment that comes with ownership will contribute to the success of a project. Recognize that members of a project team are inclined to have a stronger commitment to the team if they feel their participation and contributions are valued. Understand the business. Be able to pass judgment on issues under consideration and reach a firm decision. And finally, experienced project managers increase the odds of success.

In addition to leadership skills and project management experience, all projects need some kind of forecast for return on investment (ROI). Project and program estimating is little more than predicting the future outcome of a project or program. It is a hard and unwieldy undertaking. There are really only two kinds of estimates: lucky or lousy. These estimates are often made by different people, at different times, using different methods. More standards for estimating could produce significant improvements; however, there is a caution. Project managers must realize that using function points, lines of code, and computing hours of coding time as metrics for developing applications are techniques that are approaching buggy-whip status and are now nearly useless.

Chart 5

1994 - 2004 Average Percent of Features & Functions
(Resolved Projects)

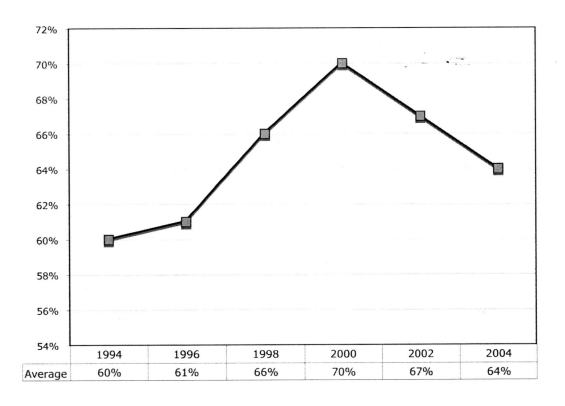

	1994	1996	1998	2000	2002	2004
Average	60%	61%	66%	70%	67%	64%

Source: CHAOS Database, surveys conducted 1994 thru 2004

Lesson Seven looks at the financial aspects of software development projects, condensed into the following 10 points: Create and maintain accurate estimates and develop a more systematic approach toward project estimating and costing. Know that projects are marathons, so prepare for the long run. Look at ways to make your project more financially attractive. Consider working with a project budget and understand how companies manage their information technology money. Know the elusive financial break-even point and how that point changes as the project moves forward. Manage change; failure to do so is almost always a major contributor to project failure. Use incentives to finish the project as a way to improve success and reduce failures. Don't be afraid to kill a project and take your lumps and losses. Recognize the benefits of pruning or re-factoring your code — cutting out unused or meaningless code. And finally, create a functional pipeline.

Just as important as financial management is assembling and managing the skilled resources needed to complete a project. In their book Contented Cows Give Better Milk (Williford Communications, 2000), authors Bill Catlette and Richard Hadden explain how keeping employees happy leads to better profits and an improved bottom line. Some of the things Catlette and Hadden recommend are truthfulness, training, and communication. These all are cornerstones to having and maintaining skilled resources. Certainly a better working environment should increase productivity. And increased productivity can increase velocity of software application development stepping-stones, which in turn will lead to more successful projects and systems. However, you should not confuse activity with progress. Progress is achieved through skilled and competent teamwork.

Lesson Eight on skilled resources addresses the major issues of managing an application development staff, and the issues around their support systems. The lesson covers the following 10 points: Examine the matter of competency and what you need to consider in evaluating the competency of your staff and the team. Place workers with skills in jobs that will most benefit the project. Use incentives as a tool to motivate achievement of project goals or significant stepping-stones. Look at team building and keeping the team together. Establish staff development and training programs. Make use of mentors and mentoring to improve the skills and competency of staff members and the team. Consider the role of "chemistry" among team members and how it can affect the project in both positive and negative ways. Learn what you can do when the chemistry does not work and you have an exceptionally difficult team member.

Recognize the effects of turnover on projects and find ways to deal with it. And the last point comes from Foster Schucker, CTO of Kaloke Technologies, and his theory for successful projects through skilled staff.

With a skilled staff in place, project leaders may consider the use of a formal methodology. This is simply a way of doing things, a method of action. In recent years, project management professionals have tried to put more flesh on this skeleton and define it in more elaborate terms.

A methodology is a set of policies, procedures, standards, processes, practices, tools, techniques, and tasks that practitioners apply to technical and management challenges. It is used to manage the deployment of technology with work plans, requirements documents, and test plans. It is also used to deploy technology. A formal methodology could include coding standards, code libraries, development practices, and much more.

Lesson Nine on formal methodology starts with a look at formal versus informal project methodology, and goes on to cover what should be included in a formal methodology, condensed into the following 10 points: A formal methodology must have a problem statement to ensure that everyone is solving the same business problem. Establish a formal process for gathering and maintaining requirements. Develop a detailed project plan. Understand that one missed small detail can cause big problems that could lead to project failure — the "butterfly effect." Consider the use of analogies to improve communication between users and developers. Maintain a formal methodology to support interaction between stakeholders. This point includes a case study on how a formal methodology improved the results in hospital intensive care units. Consider the concept of the Project Management Office (PMO). Integrate formal peer reviews into your formal process. This point examines the British Central Government's OGC Gateway Process. And finally, employ a flexible formal process to improve the success rate.

As part of a formal methodology, the purpose of any tool should be to support the project management process. However, you should realize tools do not control an individual project's outcome. I have four suggestions to assist you in using project management tools more effectively: Communicate, communicate, communicate, and

Chart 6

Percent of ROI Calculated by Project Resolution

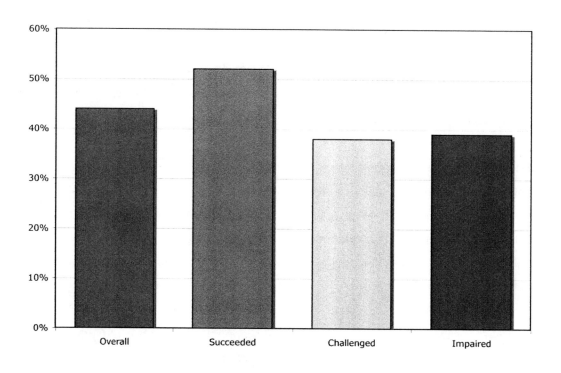

Source: CHAOS Database survey results, 2004

when that's finished, communicate some more. Understand that communication is the most crucial aspect of a project.

The last lesson on tools and infrastructure starts with a look at a project toolkit and the types of tools you will need to manage and control your project or projects. It covers the following points: Your toolkit should have a standard vocabulary to facilitate proper communications. The use of requirements management tools can have a huge impact on the success of a project. Change management software has many benefits in the dynamic world of developing application software. Consider a collaboration tool like WebEx, especially for distributed and geographically dispersed teams. Use inspection and testing tools like you would use spell check on documents — application software bugs are the leading cause of downtime. Consider the benefits of a standard infrastructure, and how it helped a company like Sprint. Learn how to recognize trustworthy and untrustworthy vendors. Consider the benefits of using open source software and components to jump-start a project and provide the baseline. This point includes a case study on how Standish Group created a major software product using this technique. The last point is to use cost, risk, and gain as the central factors to optimizing your project portfolio and requirements set.

You will find several themes repeated throughout these pages: Communications and simplicity are keys to successful projects. Scope and requirements are typically over specified. Money is the root of all evil, and time is the enemy of all projects.

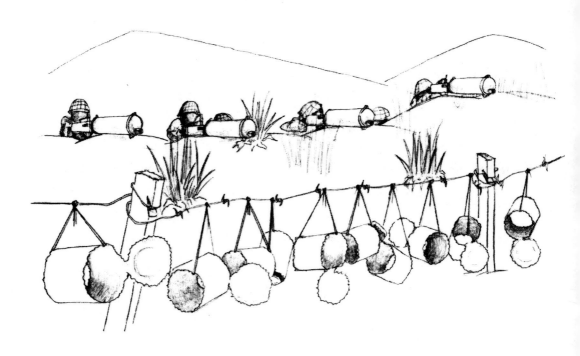

Lesson One: Guadalcanal

At midnight on October 25, 1942, on Guadalcanal, the Imperial Japanese Army attacked the U.S. Marines who were defending Henderson Field, the island's air base. The Marine's defense was a line of water-cooled machine guns. About 100 feet from their position, the Marines set up wires with cans attached. Far away, the Marines could hear the Japanese advancing, but they kept still. When the Japanese tripped over the wires and the cans rattled, the Marines fired their machine guns with 900 rounds per minute. The battle ended three hours later. The Japanese were defeated. Only one American was wounded - 26-year-old Marine Gunnery Sergeant "Manila John" Basilone.

The M1917 fired bullets so fast that the barrel would melt from the heat. The original design of the rapid-fire gun shot 450 rounds per minute. However, the rapid fire caused the machine gun to vibrate. The vibration impaired accuracy and at 1,000 feet, the gun would fire 9 feet from the target. Since the M1917 was mainly a defensive weapon, long-range accuracy was crucial. On Guadalcanal, Sergeant Basilone realized this problem and reengineered the weapon to reduce the vibration. In doing so, he also increased the shots per minute from 450 to 900. Such rapid fire caused the Japanese to think that there were many more Marines at Henderson Field than there really were. As a user of the M1917, Sergeant Basilone was intimately involved.

The redesign of the M1917 was successful because the user was involved. This is a lesson all project managers can learn from.

Point 1: Identification

For any project to succeed, it is crucial to first correctly identify the proper user.

"Users think IT is too slow and too expensive," said David Ratcliffe of ARCO. Well, if it's the project manager you want the users to respect, the project manager and the project team have to respect the user in turn. The user is the project's real client and without the user, the project has no purpose. Poorly accepted feedback by the development team can undermine performance and create resentment.

"One of the first lessons I learned about new product development is that it is crucial to include customers and advisers in that process," said CHAOS University attendee Ellen Hancock, a long-time industry professional who served executive stints at IBM, Apple, and Exodus. Standish Group's user involvement workshops at the first CHAOS University strongly endorsed the need to identify the correct user, involve the user early and often, create and maintain a quality relationship, make involvement easy, and have a clear idea of the users' needs.

CHAOS University workgroup attendees agreed that working with the correct user or group of users is just as important as user involvement. They also determined that finding this user is difficult. It is not enough to take a user's "word" for it. It must be clear that this user represents the opinions of the complete user base, and not just his or her own agenda. One workshop attendee stated that her group always assigned a full-time user to be present for every meeting. This person basically left the user community and worked full-time on the project. While most in the group agreed this was a good idea, there was concern that if a user worked too closely with IT, he or she might become too much "like an IT person." The concern was that user issues would be forgotten. Thus, everyone agreed that users involved in a project need to bring forth the opinions of the entire user community. That is why it is important to identify the proper user(s) to participate.

Point 2: Rapport

It is critical to develop and maintain a quality relationship with the user and user groups.

Attendees of CHAOS University determined that the need to understand the user's business and to communicate effectively with the user, are key to establishing a quality relationship. To determine whether a quality relationship has been established, you need to think about the following five things: First, you must create an environment with ground rules for effective teamwork. Second, the IT team has to be able to understand the user's basic business. Third, there has to be a method for managing expectations through interplay between IT and the user community. This should include negotiating and establishing formal or informal contracts, and ensuring that the rules of interplay are clearly understood. Fourth, the team should hold regular progress meetings involving the user. Last, you need to establish quality metrics and publish them to chart project progress and ongoing operations.

Once you have established a quality relationship, the next requirement is to maintain it by making it easy for users to be involved. To determine whether or not involvement has been made easy, consider these issues: The IT team must understand the user's business enough to communicate effectively with the user community. IT should refrain from using too much technical jargon so communication is clearly understood. The IT team should be proactive in soliciting user opinions. Make certain the users know what is expected of them as part of the team. Make sure the users feel their opinions make a difference. Demonstrate to the users that their views are being addressed. Make sure there is a benefit for the users to be involved and that they see this benefit.

The last point of the workshop discussion—and an important factor in the overall success of obtaining user involvement—was uncovering the users' needs. The IT team must listen to learn and learn to listen. "Find out what the users need, not what they want—there is a big difference," said Randy Smerik, president and CEO of Tarari, a hardware acceleration company based in San Diego.

Point 3: Soapbox

To maintain a quality relationship with the users, create a platform for communications.

If the users and user groups have an easy and straightforward method of communication, the more apt they will be to use it. There are several ways to set up a user communication platform, and it has never been easier, cheaper, and quicker to do so.

Electronic communications and collaboration tools, such as WebEx, allow teams to share plans and demonstrate prototypes right at a user's desk. Conference calling services can connect people from various locations. Some project management tools can automatically send notifications to stakeholders upon completion of major tasks and missed stepping-stones (a later lesson talks about the difference between stepping-stones and milestones). Online forums and discussion groups can be easily formed to get feedback on features and requirements.

Yet with all these communications channels available, projects still fail because of poor communication, little or no collaboration, and lack of user involvement. In the spring of 2004, a major British government project failed because the project team decided not to involve the users since they were too diverse and geographically scattered. In another case, a large manufacturer built a new system from the vision of the executive supporter and did not bring the users into the discussion until the training exercise. The users, who were by the way their clients, refused to use the system and walked out of the training course. The project was canceled and the organization lost several million dollars.

It should be recognized that the faster the communication, the better the results. For example, in Extreme Programming (XP) users are embedded into the development process. It is a key ingredient for XP success. What makes this technique so powerful is that the communication line between the developers and the users is very short-it is a direct link. This direct communication link saves an enormous amount of time for the developers and the project as a whole. Again, remember that time is the enemy of all projects.

Point 4: Outcomes

It is important to demonstrate results along the way.

"When we rolled the big conversion out, it met most of the technical objectives, but when the users saw it they were disappointed. We didn't have user involvement throughout the project," said Mike Prince of Burlington Coat Factory.

Once you have taken the steps to clearly identify the user base through interviews with experienced, motivated, and respected individuals who clearly understand the problem, structure the project in stages in order to gain constant feedback. This project structure provides for early-demonstrated results.

In one Standish Group engagement, the organization had not experienced a successful project in 30 years. In fact, it had not even seen a "challenged" project in 30 years. (Standish defines a challenged project as completed and/or operational, but over budget, late, or both, with fewer features and functions than originally specified.) The organization hired a new CIO and he, in turn, hired a highly motivated and experienced team of project leaders, with a history of success. They knew they needed to achieve a big project win—believing that success, on a large scale, would prove they could deliver what the company needed.

The organization's old systems truly needed to be replaced, so the team began there. However, the organization's long-standing methods made achieving a big win impossible. The group needed to try a different strategy.

Standish Group research has proven that small projects are more successful, so we focused on this point as the main key to their future success. The project team broke the larger project plan into smaller, more achievable stepping-stones with true measures of success—visual and usable pieces of the technology solution that the users could begin to use and thus perceive the benefits.

The first pieces the team delivered were not amazing, and in fact, the users didn't even find them very useful. But the project team got feedback on the first stepping-stone, corrected the issues, and went back to the users. Little by little, the pieces of the puzzle started to come together and these small "wins" helped build more confidence in IT on the part of the users.

Methodologies like Extreme Programming and Scrum both have a very short time to deliver early code, one week to a month. The reason is to demonstrate results.

Point 5: Schooling

Users and user groups need to understand their roles and responsibilities as part of the project team.

The user knows the corporation's business better than any other member of the team. This person holds an authoritative position, but also has the knowledge, and should have the mandate, to drill down into all key user departments for essential details about how the organization works.

No task is more important for the user and user groups than goal definition. Goal definition is twofold. First, the user or user group must take a detailed snapshot of the organization at the moment before project planning commences; then the user or user group must have a thorough understanding of what the user organization wants tomorrow.

The users involved must be business and/or process operational people. Operational knowledge is of utmost importance, as the users must be able to answer operational questions as they arise. The user role must be clearly determined, with specific responsibility and ownership, but it also must have a well-understood limited scope of responsibility. The users do not own the technology, they do not control or schedule the project resources, and they do not determine the approach to the project. However, they do speak with a loud voice for all user departments in matters of whether the proposed solution meets the business needs set out in the project charter.

The users should be the subject matter experts on the team. As such, they are best qualified to become the project's evangelists — selling the benefits of the project internally to the user community. If they understand the process and feel comfortable with it, the better they will be in the execution of the project and its tasks.

If the project team is deploying an agile process, it is very important to educate the users in the process. An agile process works best when decisions are made rapidly, without drawn-out analysis. An agile process works poorly, as do most projects, when decisions stagnate.

Point 6: Consensus

Gather user feedback and achieve consensus.

Admiral Chester Nimitz's rules of thumb stated: First, is the proposed operation likely to succeed? Second, what are the consequences of failure? And third, is it practical in terms of material and supplies?" said industry veteran Ellen Hancock at CHAOS University 1995. "These are not bad rules to evaluate a new project."

So the key question is, how do you optimize support to contribute to successful projects? In Hancock's experience there are two main factors to success: first, internal and external input as well as support; second, excellence in project management techniques and processes.

When Hancock served as a senior executive at IBM, she utilized two primary techniques to ensure the development process incorporated the users' and outside consultants' views. First, IBM established an industry council, which met twice a year. IBM shared strategies, development plans, and market introductions with this council. The company found these sessions to be extremely successful and could make major changes in direction based on feedback from the council.

Second, IBM linked customer councils to product commitment. Customers would review product plans at all stages of development. IBM would get feedback based on real customer knowledge and experience. By doing this, IBM developed products that the customer needed. This greatly reduced the risk of bringing a product to market that did not meet customer demand.

Another crucial element of project success is to ensure consensus among the team members as well as buy-in from the project's lead executive. A sure sign of buy-in is when the executive becomes the project spokesperson. If you have an executive sponsor who is not willing to be the spokesperson, you have an executive who has not bought in to the project. As Hewlett-Packard's former president John Young stated, "Successful companies have a consensus from top to bottom on a set of overall goals. The most brilliant management strategy will fail if that consensus is missing."

Keys to project management include small, cross-functional teams with experience, honest views of external realities, solid design and architecture, and links to customer demand.

Point 7: Evangelist

All projects need to identify and recruit an evangelist.

Projects that have users or user groups who zealously evangelize and disseminate the project's value throughout the organization score better in Standish Research project evaluations than those that do not. In essence, evangelism, a form of marketing, is a very intense style of communication. As mentioned earlier, the greater the degree of communication among parties, the greater the chance of success. Projects in which the user or user groups score well as evangelists have a higher success rate. Projects in which the user or user groups have a fair to poor rating as evangelists have a lower success rate.

The kind of person who makes a good evangelist is one who generally has a pleasant outlook and a positive attitude. The person must have credibility with the rest of the organization to be able influence their opinions. In Malcom Gladwell's book The Tipping Point (Little, Brown, 2000), he discusses "connectors." Connectors are people who know lots of people and everyone knows them. A connector who has a positive view of the project and credibility with the organization would be a great evangelist. A connector who does not have either could be a problem.

Step one is to identify possible evangelists. So make a list, check it twice, and think about who would be naughty or nice! Step two is to engage them as primary user representatives. Step three is to make sure they understand how valuable the project is to the organization and the benefits it has to them and their peers. The key is WIIFM — What's In It For Me? When selling the project to a possible evangelist you must consider the benefits, both personal and professional, it will bring to him or her.

Once you have an evangelist in your fold, you need to nurture him or her, keep him informed on progress, bounce ideas and issues off him, and solicit advice and counsel. "The importance of constant communications, managing people so they follow through, and getting people involved early are lessons I learned the hard way," said Mark Palmer, project manager, Concordia University.

Chart 7

How often do you run focus groups to discover
user needs and requirements?

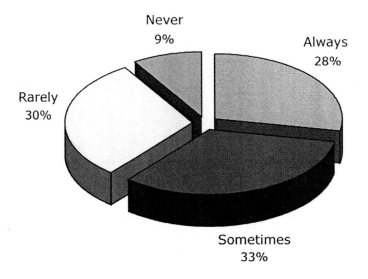

Source: DARTS May 2006

Point 8: Primary Research

Project leaders must understand why and how to conduct primary research.

First, consider primary research as virgin research. In other words, it is research conducted directly by the organization that has not been done before. However, primary research can also be research that has been done before, but is now being updated with new instruments and techniques. "The only thing sacred in our company is the user," said Ken Edwards of Ameritech. "We do focus groups, interviews, and demonstrations to ensure we meet the users' needs. No one in our company talks about internal standards or restricted products. It is all about the user."

Standish Group has a three-step process to gain valuable information: interviews, focus groups, and surveys. We start with the key individuals to gain insight into the vision and areas of concern. We use this information to build the moderator guide for focus groups. We love focus groups and we do lots of them. It is a great way to get user feedback and build consensus. It is also a simple and inexpensive way to dig deep to get the high-value items. You need to execute a minimum of three to get a cross-sectional view. We follow up those focus groups with a Web-based closed-end survey.

To determine whether or not you have researched your user group's needs effectively, ask yourself if the following statements are true: You have conducted the primary research to uncover the users' or user group's needs and requirements via interviews, focus groups, and interviews. You have built a consensus with the users on the vision of the project and how it will benefit them. The users and user groups have been involved and agree with the requirement documents and prototypes. You have an understanding of the priority by features and functions. You have in place a feedback system to communicate changes as the project progresses.

Point 9: Respect

Never fail to show respect for users. You need them to provide constant information and feedback to the project team.

If the users would just tell us what they really want, it would be easier to give it to them," said Karim Raad, formerly of Cornerstone Software. If only it were that easy. Often, users cannot articulate what they want, and the team misinterprets their requirements. Or, the IT members create emotional barriers to the users expressing themselves fully, by making them feel like "dumb users." All too often, users are not forthcoming because of these emotional barriers.

Project managers and the project team can create an environment that encourages and welcomes user input and involvement. First, insist on frequent, accurate, specific, and timely information. Conduct user status meetings often, building requirements and feedback into meetings. Second, create both formal and informal methods to provide information to the project team. Third, respect the users' opinions and the information they provide. They have to live with what is created when you go on to bigger and better things.

Often the user or user groups will understand their own narrow business or process operational requirements, the so-called "stove-piped" departments, but lack knowledge or understanding of how those requirements fit into the overall business. Projects that involve users who have an understanding of their functions within the context of the overall business score better in Standish Group research than projects involving users who do not possess this knowledge.

One of the most important advancements over the years of Standish Group research has been the expanded definition of "user." Initially, an "end user" was just the user of the system or process. The definition has expanded to include all customers and stakeholders. "The problem I have with the term 'user involvement' is it centers on the end user, when what you really need is everyone with a stake in the outcome of the project. This could include audit, taxation, compliance, regulators, or anyone who uses the output of the system," said Suzanne McGugan, formerly of BMO Financial Group.

Clearly, the thinking on user involvement has evolved. The following quote came from the original 1994 Standish Group CHAOS Report, when the project success rate was 16 percent: "Brain-dead users, just plain brain-dead users," said Peter, an application analyst at a bank.

Point 10: True Grit

Focus on the real user needs. It is one of the most important factors in the overall success of a project.

In study after study, Standish Group has concluded that a very minor portion of the features and functions built ever get used in production. Consider the universal 80/20 rule, which states that 80 percent of the benefit will come from 20 percent of the features and functions. Standish Group has concluded that the practice of gathering all the requirements upfront and searching for hidden needs produces products in which the average use of features and functions is only 17 percent. On the other hand, if you focus on reducing scope to the essential requirements, the usage percent will rise substantially.

Projects in which users or user groups have a good understanding of their true needs have a better rate of return and lower risk than those that have broader requirements. On average, projects in which users or user groups pushed for more and more features and functions fell into both "challenged" and "failed" categories. Scope equals time, and time, again, is the enemy of all projects.

Surprisingly, many users are not skilled at conveying what they need, nor do they understand how getting what they need will benefit them. It is a given that the project will produce a result; however, that result may or may not be a consequence of the users knowing what they originally needed or wanted. Gordon Divitt, former CEO of FundServ, said, "Users will often get what they ask for even if they didn't know they asked for it."

It is easier for IT to understand the true user needs if users are involved, happy, and committed. But even if the users state what their needs are, does IT truly understand what those needs mean? Moreover, can IT get the users to differentiate between needs and wants? The IT team must listen to learn and learn to listen. "Find out what the users need, not what they want—there is a big difference," said Randy Smerik of Tarari.

In Conclusion

Users and user groups must have the ability to explain the business process in detail to the IT organization, and those users should be trained to follow project management protocols. Successful projects include users with good communication skills. Challenged and failed projects typically include users with fair to poor communication skills.

Of all the attributes of a project, realism, or the lack thereof, produces the starkest contrast in outcomes. Users must be aware of the limitations that are imposed on the project. For example, project developers cannot be expected to produce miraculous results of functionality in a short amount of time if resources are restricted. Users and user groups that are realistic have higher success rates; they have an inclination toward pragmatism, which in turn cam minimize project risk.

So let us review the 10 points of user involvement. Point 1 covered how to correctly identify the proper user. Point 2 discussed the importance of developing and maintaining a quality relationship with the user and user groups. Point 3 stressed that project teams need to create and maintain a platform for communications in order to have a quality relationship with the users. Point 4 discussed the importance of demonstrating results. Point 5 talked about educating the users on the project management process and their roles and responsibilities within the process. Point 6 discussed gathering user feedback and achieving consensus. Point 7 talked about how to identify and recruit an evangelist. Point 8 covered primary research—why and how to conduct it. Point 9 stressed the importance of showing respect for users. The last point focused on separating real user needs from wants.

In a 1999 Standish Group focus group we asked, "Do you manage projects differently now than a year ago?" A great deal of the participants said they get the user more involved in all levels of the project phases—planning, development, and implementation. History has shown that establishing and maintaining quality user participation is the most important lesson for project managers. Those who ignore this lesson are destined to have poor results.

Lesson Two: Remember the Alamo

"We will give them no quarter," announced General Antonio Lopez de Santa Anna of the Mexican army. In 1836 a small band of 189 gallant but disorganized freedom fighters held 2,000 highly trained Mexican dragoons at bay for 13 days. Day after day the cannons pounded away at the Alamo, a fragile, ill-made church fort. Commander William Travis sent out pleas for reinforcements to Sam Houston, a leader of the independence movement and commander in chief of the Texas rebels. Houston was in the process of drafting the Texas constitution and did not support their cause. He did not send help to the besieged patriots.

Finally, concerned that Houston would indeed send reinforcements, General Santa Anna gave the order for the Mexicans to overrun what he called the "land pirates." The battle started at 5:30 a.m. March 6, 1836, and ended before the sun rose. All Alamo defenders perished, including Davy Crockett and Jim Bowie. This is a dramatic example of how the lack of executive management support can destroy a project.

It is crucial that the executive has a vested business interest and a commitment to a successful outcome. Most successful projects have quality executive sponsors with expert vision and prompt responsiveness. Challenged and failed projects typically lack quality executive support. In most cases, projects without quality executive support will perform poorly. The following 10 points discuss the attributes of quality executive sponsorship.

Point 1: Simple Vision

Develop and maintain a clear and simple vision statement; it is imperative to the overall success of any project.

When President John F. Kennedy said the nation would put a man on the moon within a decade, it was a clear and simple vision. Getting there was a different story, however — the space program was complex, with hundreds of projects. But the greatest thing Kennedy's vision did was to put everyone at NASA on the same page, without any ambiguity. A clear and simple vision statement coming from the executive sponsor is a leading precondition for project success. Of course, like most things in life, this is easier said than done.

Standish Group suggests that a concise definition of the project vision should be written when developing the requirements. The definition should have the following attributes: First, it should be written in the context and language of the business, not in IT terms. Second, the vision should encompass project benefits for the short, mid, and long term of the project's life cycle, and it should be communicated, and agreed to, by all project stakeholders. Third, it should be tied to the overall corporate vision and strategy. Fourth, it should be concise and to the point. Fifth, it should include a statement of participation and the roles of the stakeholders. Sixth, if the project warrants, it could include a request for support and a commitment to contribution.

Once you have a project vision, the stakeholders must buy into it. First, you need to test the understanding and commitment of the stakeholder by asking them, "What is the vision?" In Standish Group's "group therapy" sessions, this is the first question we ask. We have the delegates to the session write down in three simple words the objective of the project. We then work on building a consensus and tying their understanding back to the vision statement. Second, once all stakeholders agree on the vision, you ask for a commitment of participation. Third, the executive sponsor needs to recognize the stakeholders' contribution.

Chart 8

How often do you have both the users and the key executive sponsor approve the requirements?

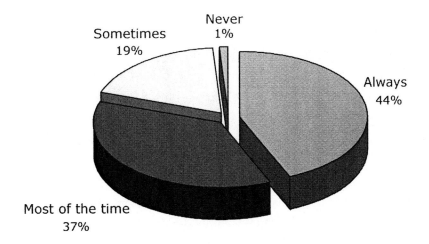

Source: DARTS September 2005

Point 2: Commitment

It is crucial that the executive has a vested business interest and a commitment to a successful outcome.

In order to ensure this business interest and commitment, you must first understand the organization, the role of the executive within this organization, and what factors motivate this individual to become a champion of the project. "If management doesn't get it, get new management," said Phil Schaadt, former CIO of Bank of America. This might be easier said than done from the project manager's standpoint.

Even so, you must clearly understand the organization's business issues and what will motivate the executive to support the project. Identify the political issues that affect the executive and find ways to capitalize on them. Make sure that the executive who supports the project will gain stature from a successful project.

"If you can find six customers who think you are wonderful and will put down their hard dollars, I will fund the project," said industry veteran and former IBM executive Ellen Hancock at a CHAOS University session. Hancock made her commitment based on the commitment of her customers. Judy Wright of Royal Bank of Canada seconded Hancock's remarks at CHAOS University: "We have an owner for every application we support, and they have monetary incentives for the success of the project."

Money shows a commitment, but it is only one part of the equation. Another part of the equation, which is sometimes harder to get from an executive sponsor, is time. The executive champion needs to spend time with the stakeholders and participants to foretell the vision and highlight the benefits the project will bring to the organization. Time is the enemy of projects, and lack of executive time is the greatest foe.

Another part of the equation is influence. If the executive sponsor has influence, he or she can use that influence to gain and direct essential resources needed to accomplish the project. A highly connected executive sponsor could mean the difference between success and failure. The executive sponsor should be committed to use this influence to ensure the health of the project.

The executive sponsor must be willing to take risks and stand by his or her commitment to the project in the face of risk. "Even as a small company, we are a risk-taker and leader in adopting new technology," said Robert Gibson of Visiting Nurse Health System.

Point 3: Blink

While thinking is clearly necessary, and important, don't spend too much time doing it!

On a flight back from London, I struck up a conversation with the segment manager of a large professional consulting group who was seated beside me. I soon learned that his organization is focused on implementing customer resource management (CRM) solutions. Our conversation segued into a discussion about the latest CHAOS body of knowledge, to which he related two engagements.

The first was his current assignment: the implementation of a CRM for a large pharmaceutical company. The engagement had been going on for three years, with no end in sight. It was classic CHAOS: There was no senior-level support, IT was building a gold-plated infrastructure, and the users were bored out their minds. He commented that despite all the danger signs, management would not yield because the consulting company was getting paid big fees. Internally, the pharmaceutical company's lower-level managers would not rock the boat for fear of losing their jobs.

The other engagement we discussed was a CRM application for another large pharmaceutical company. In this case, there was a drop-dead end date of four months. If the CRM was not installed within this time frame, the company would be forced to close its doors. The reason for this dramatic event is beyond the scope of this book, but it truly was a hard stop date. In any case, the entire company was focused on successfully installing the application. Senior management took an active role and made decisions quickly and without looking back. In the end, all the salespeople were brought together for their training on the new live system two weeks before the drop-dead date.

The book I chose to bring with me as reading material for that same European trip was Blink: The Power of Thinking without Thinking (Little, Brown & Company, 2005), by Malcolm Gladwell. The focus of this book is on "thin slicing," or making faster decisions based on unconscious thinking and intuitive knowledge. This well-written book could change your mind about how to make important decisions. The point I am trying to make is that time is the enemy of all projects—and that includes thinking time.

Point 4: Velocity

Fast decision-making requires a decision pipeline.

In Gladwell's book Blink, there are two particularly memorable examples. One is regarding Cook County Hospital and the other concerns war games conducted by the U.S. government. In the Cook County Hospital example, the author showed how too much examination does not help to make better decisions, and may actually cause more harm than good. In the war games example, a team that made rapid gut reactions beat a larger, more equipped, and methodical group in short order. In these Blink examples, decisions that were made "in a blink" were much more effective than those made using drawn-out analysis. What the decision makers also did was increase the velocity of decisions as well as the speed of completion to an end result.

"Quick resolution in order to move on with the business of business is key," said Tobey Marzouk of Marzouk & Parry, a Washington, D.C. law firm specializing in failed projects. Success of any project depends on the commitment of management and its understanding of the project priorities. Preventing any hindrance to progress or production is paramount.

There is always a tightrope between the expressions "ready, fire, aim" and "paralysis through analysis." Certainly, rapidly made bad decisions could be worse than slowly made good decisions, but they often have the same consequences. The utopia is expeditious skilled resolutions. Every project will have a certain amount of bad and good decisions; which type is more plentiful makes the difference between a successful project and an unsuccessful one. If time is the enemy of all projects, then too much time spent thinking and not enough time doing is deadly.

The best way to encourage rapid decision-making is to present the executives with a clear and concise set of alternatives: If we do "A" this will happen; if we do "B" this is the likely outcome. Another way is to create a framework for decision-making that doesn't involve the executive, and just notify him or her as decisions are made. The strategy is to keep the project moving at a rapid pace, yet keep the executive(s) involved.

Point 5: Edification

Once a project has the backing of the right executive sponsor, it's vital to educate him or her on the project management process and his or her role and responsibilities.

Since the executive sponsor is the prime visionary and has a global view of the project, he or she must illustrate how the project supports corporate goals and thus benefits the organization. The executive sponsor sets the agenda, arranges the funding, and articulates the project's overall objective. He or she is the project's champion, and the project lives and dies by the executive sponsor. Therefore, it is important to educate the executive sponsor on your process.

Projects in which the executive sponsor has a good understanding of the project management methodology have a better chance for success than those projects for which this understanding on the part of the executive is absent. Projects in which the executive sponsor has a fair to poor understanding of the project management process fall into both the "challenged" and "failed" categories. As with users, a basic tutorial on the project management process for executive sponsors will help in the success of the project.

Through education you can encourage the executive sponsor to champion the project by having clear escalation processes for resolving project risks and expense issues. You should provide full disclosure and educate the sponsor on how you will minimize blindsiding with a clear and concise plan and a reporting system. Educate the sponsor on your well-defined goals and stepping-stones and demonstrate how you focus on business. You should streamline the reporting system so that you have direct access to the executive sponsor. "Bad news never travels well," said David Bicknell, staff writer of ComputerWeekly. This may be true, but you want bad news to travel fast so corrective action can happen without delays. Remember, time is the enemy.

Fear of failure can either propel or paralyze, depending on the consequences. In most cases, it is not the ideal motivator because it will either push people to take unnecessary risks, or make them so cautious that they impede progress. Great strides can be made when the opportunity to fail, for valid reasons, coexists peacefully with the opportunity to succeed.

Point 6: Measurements

Successful project completion is contingent upon reaching specified goals. Use those goals, which include time lines, budgets, and features/functions, as a yardstick for measuring if the project is on track.

"Many executives think that the IT department oversells its capabilities and under-delivers," said Gordon Divitt, These executives have come to expect that project failures are a cost of doing business. This has proven to be dangerous ground for executive sponsors. In rare but rapidly increasing cases, where the executive sponsor has an IT background, technology skills can be a plus. However, the executive sponsor may only have enough knowledge to be harmful. Projects where the executive sponsor has a reasonable knowledge of technology fare better than those that do not.

"From the inception, how you craft the deal and how you decide what you want and what you don't want determines whether your project will fail or not," noted Tobey Marzouk of Marzouk & Parry. The objective of a project is the successful implementation and use of the product. However, it is a consequence of business that disputes arise around issues or shortcomings, such as the project does not meet a promised delivery date or an important feature or function was excluded. If, in the end, the product does not work properly, or the users don't want it, it is a failure.

Oftentimes, quarrels involve two traditionally disparate parties — typically the user community and the IT development group — each with their own agenda and definitions of progress. "Clear standards of measuring the deliverables are the best way of proceeding," Marzouk stated. The most important step in deciding project requirements is obtaining user input on written business processes and requirements. This procedure should not be disregarded. A solid understanding of user requirements helps to define application capabilities throughout the project's life cycle. User-specified features and functions must serve as the baseline for all basic requirements in the design phase.

"We sit down and ask, 'What are we going to do and who's going to do it?' If there is a big silence, there's a good sign there is a gap," said Divitt.

Point 7: Negotiate

Putting together a successful project plan requires negotiation.

"Information is at the heart of the matter," cites Herb Cohen, author of You Can Negotiate Anything (L. Stuart, 1980) and keynote speaker at the joint CHAOS University/Project Leadership Conference in March 2002. Being in the IT business, it certainly is at the heart of our matter. While Cohen talks in generalities about techniques in negotiations, there are many take-aways that can be applied to your own circumstances. His philosophies and words of wisdom can be applied at the program and project level. The following is the kind of information you might need to negotiate a successful project plan.

First, understand the informal power structure of the organization. Go beyond the title and placement within the organizational chart to understand where the real work gets done. Make sure you know who can really make decisions and what kinds of decisions they can make. Know how the power translates from one organization to another. It's important to ask simple questions such as, Do the developers dictate technology? Or do decisions come from above via an executive or technical office?

Second, be aware of the true time frame of a project. This knowledge will provide a great deal of information that will help to negotiate a winning project plan. For example, if there is a project that needs to be in place within five months because of market conditions and/or corporate commitment, that is a firm time frame. However, if project managers know that the IT department estimates that the project as it is specified will take nine months to complete, they also know that the two sides need to come to an understanding. Cohen says there are two types of outcomes: collaborative or adversarial. A collaborative outcome will make both sides happy, while an adversarial outcome typically makes just one side happy—but in many, if not most cases, both sides will feel cheated.

Third, understand the need—not just the expressed need, but the true need. In Standish Group's study on features actually used in the average mission-critical application, we found that only 17 percent of the features and functions developed were used. Knowing the true needs and the motivation for those needs could go a long way toward negotiating a successful project plan and execution.

Point 8: The Plan

A project plan must be well thought out and well articulated to all parties involved, particularly the executive sponsor.

A good plan will help to convince the executive sponsor you are on target, and that will help to gain his or her support. The plan should include these four items: It should define stepping-stones to identify early signs of success. It should show the executive sponsor the potential benefits to justify the investment and risk. It should include a contingency plan, which is conveyed to the executive. It should include a kill switch, and the executive should know how to use it.

"In seeking executive management support, a well-devised plan will go a long way in gaining executive management buy-in. We had to market the incremental project results and success to the executive sponsors so they would feel encouraged and positive about the project," said Jason Feinman of the U.S. Postal Service.

Tobey Marzouk of Marzouk & Parry suggests that after the requirements are determined, the project leader should ensure that development efforts remain consistent with these requirements. Adhering to design specifications has several beneficial side effects. First, it streamlines the development effort by eliminating unnecessary or stray components. Second, it identifies a unique function ahead of time so the development team is prepared. Third, it reveals how various project elements interact. And fourth, it delivers basic features and functions quickly.

In order to determine whether your plan will positively influence executive management, you need to do the following: Communicate project costs, revenues, enhancements, and strategic necessities. Communicate the risks. Communicate the commitment for the necessary people, time, and financial resources. Communicate the measurement and reporting criteria. And detail how the executive sponsor can champion and promote the project.

If the executive sponsor is an ardent defender or supporter of the project, its chances of success are higher. However, if the executive sponsor is only mildly supportive, the chances for success are less, with overruns and failure likely. A well-thought-out plan will go a long way toward gaining the executive's support.

Point 9: Kill Switch

Every project should have a kill switch. A kill switch is a predetermined position where it is unwise to continue to invest in the project.

"My boss at Blue Cross Boston asked me, 'What should I do with this $80 million project?' My reply was to blow it up. He then asked, 'How do I sell that to the board?' I told him, 'I think you need a second opinion.' So we had IBM look at it and they told him to blow it up, too," said Marty Joyce, former COO at Blue Cross Boston.

When approaching the executive to obtain buy-in, expect concerns about failure. The way to minimize these concerns is through a kill switch. Focus on minimizing the investment by creating stepping-stones. Stepping-stones are like milestones, except that milestone are more date focused. Stepping-stones are concrete deliverables and give you the ability to demonstrate results.

Many organizations hesitate to use a kill switch. "So, each time we got into trouble we had to go to management to review the business case. It was the right thing to do." Martin Cobb, formerly of the Treasury Board of Canada Secretariat, said, "Many times we were in a position to stop a bad project, but the project had proceeded to such an extent that there was lots of support for it. It was like trying to stop a runaway locomotive with a red flag." Dan Horsey of the IRS confirmed Cobb's opinion. "Our project was full of danger signs. It is really important for an organization to step back and look at it objectively." Clear stepping-stones minimize failures and make these potential failures less troublesome.

In should be noted that organizations should not shy away from risky projects. An organization that has no failures will never be a leader in the marketplace, since it is not pushing its technology fast or far enough. A kill switch lets you do risky projects while minimizing losses. In fact, it could step up the amount of projects. To paraphrase Thomas Edison, "The secret to success is failing fast."

Point 10: Celebrate

It's important to celebrate success.

I'm not talking about holding champagne parties or taking the employees off to exotic islands in the South Seas (although in some cases this might not be a bad reward for exceptional performance). I'm talking about celebrating small wins, like reaching a stepping-stone. A kind word, a short note, a little extra bonus, or a few extra stock options can go a long way toward encouraging a team to spur on and get to that next stepping-stone. This kind of encouragement needs to come from the executive sponsor to have the maximum effect.

"The importance of constant communications, managing people so they follow through, and getting people involved early are lessons I learned the hard way," said Mark Palmer, a project manager at Concordia University. "But the real key to my project success is candy!" — with which he apparently is quite generous.

In the early days of Tandem Computers, the company had what was known as a "Beer Bust." Every Friday from about 4 p.m. to 6 p.m. employees would stop work and join together to celebrate that week's accomplishments. People from the factory, accounting, marketing, development, and executives would meet and talk informally about the company and what they had been doing that week. I am not saying there was a cause and effect here, but in fact when Tandem stopped holding the "Beer Bust" the company lost its edge.

What was so powerful about the company buying each employee a beer was the celebration, which brought about good feelings and a sense of collaboration. In this informal setting some of the best ideas were launched, gnarly problems were solved, and many gripes and grievances were neutralized.

These same good feelings and a sense of collaboration can been brought down to the project team level. If you buy into the Extreme Programming concept, then a Friday afternoon "Beer Bust" might be right for you. On the other hand, if you are a Scrum shop, holding a monthly pizza night could be more appropriate for your organization.

Regardless of how you celebrate, celebrate!

In Conclusion

Projects that have an active and responsive executive sponsor fare better than those left to hang alone without a champion. An executive sponsor who is readily available to answer, suggest, influence, and resolve appeals indicates responsiveness. Executive responsiveness increases the chances of success. The executive sponsor needs to be personally accountable to ensure a successful outcome. The greater the executive's skill in this area, the greater the chances of success. A non-responsive executive, on the other hand, increases the chances that a project will experience overruns or failure.

Now let us review the 10 points of executive sponsorship. Point 1 looked at the need for a clearly understood vision. Point 2 covered executive sponsor commitment. Point 3 stressed thinking quickly and not overanalyzing. Point 4 talked about the velocity of decision making and creating a pipeline for decisions. Point 5 discussed educating the executive sponsor on the project process. Point 6 covered using project goals and stepping-stones as measurement tools. Point 7 detailed how and why to negotiate. Point 8 covered the need to have a well-thought-out plan to convince the executive sponsor you are on target and to gain his or her support. Point 9 pointed out the benefits of a kill switch and why all projects should have one. And finally, Point 10 stressed the merits of celebration.

In addition, remember that time is the enemy of all projects. All too often, features and functions are added to a project with no understanding of the consequences of doing so. You must discourage scope creep by alerting the executive sponsor of those impacts, establish a formal change management procedure, and push to deliver on time with firm stepping-stones. The executive sponsor has the power to make tough business decisions and reduce political conflicts.

Calvin Coolidge once said, "The business of America is business." For the executive sponsor, the business of the "project" is business. The greater the understanding of the overall business goals the executive brings and communicates to the project team, the greater the probability of success. The converse is also true.

Lesson Three: Vietnam

In 1962, U.S. President John F. Kennedy committed 4,000 support troops to South Vietnam. During President Lyndon B. Johnson's term, the commitment mushroomed into a full-scale war, with more than 500,000 soldiers at its height. Using both land and air power, Commander General William C. Westmoreland set out to restrain the North Vietnamese and South Vietnamese Communists from destroying the South Vietnamese government. But Ho Chi Minh, the North Vietnamese Communist leader, with support from the Soviet Union and the Peoples' Republic of China, slowly gathered internal support and prevailed. On April 29, 1975, the South Vietnam capital, Saigon, fell to the Communists.

The Vietnam War demonstrates a classic failure in strategy. The military did not implement a strategy to win the war, but instead opted for tactics of containment, which were ineffective. The nightly news showed the horrors of the conflict. As the body count rose, support for the war declined. Through three presidents, the U.S. government could not, and did not, articulate a clear vision and strategy to the U.S. citizens.

As Yogi Berra once said, "If you don't know where you are going, you might wind up someplace else." This rings so true when it comes to a project's business objectives. Clarity and focus are essential to a successful project. The 10 points on clear business objectives in this lesson provide a foundation for your ability to construct, maintain, and adjust clear business objectives and drive the project to a successful conclusion.

Point 1: Same Page

It is imperative that everyone have the same understanding of the project's business objectives.

Standish Group has conducted more than 100 "group therapy" sessions over the years. A group therapy session is similar to a focus group or workshop, except all the participants are part of a single project team. This group generally consists of the project manager, executive sponsor, user representatives, and technical representatives of a particular project. The size of each group therapy session ranges from six to 12 people. Sessions have no more than 12 participants because group dynamics tend to get lost in larger groups. A Standish adviser moderates the group therapy session and leads the participants.

The first thing the Standish adviser asks of the participants is to write, in 10 words or less, the goal of their project. In more than 100 group therapy sessions, not one person has had the same goal as any other participant in the session. In one particular session a user wrote, "…will create a reusable object-oriented infrastructure for change," while a developer of the project wrote, "…is an update to the billing system." Not surprisingly, this project was canceled with a loss of more than $5 million to that organization. When there is no common understanding of the project, you know the project is in trouble. However, it is possible to solve half the problem right away by getting everyone on the same page.

The goals of the organization take precedence over the goals of the individual or any individual department, even the information technology department. BellSouth's Steve Sauer said, "You have to talk in the language of the business." From a business perspective, everyone has to be aligned with the direction of the overall business and the project's overall objectives. As depicted in the movie Apollo 13, U.S. citizens all bought into a shared vision of the space program, which riveted our attention on a national goal. A project's vision needs to be clear, concise, and comprehensible, but it also has to be the same to all the stakeholders. It is imperative that everyone be on the same page. Conflicting vision causes conflicts, and conflicts can cause complexity. Complexity causes confusion and cost.

Chart 9

How often do you define the project goals that would identify
the early signs of success or failure?

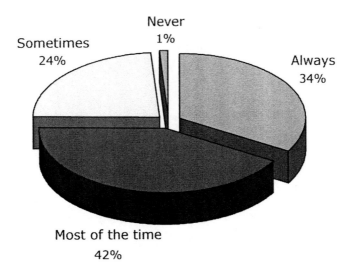

Source: DARTS September 2005

Point 2: Elevator Pitch

Business objectives need to be comprehensible and concise—they should take no longer to recite than the length of an elevator ride.

Dorothy and Toto's journey to the Land of Oz is one illustration of the power of shared objectives. When Dorothy began the trip down the Yellow Brick Road, she fully embraced the Munchkins' vision of the Emerald City and its all-powerful Wizard. When she met the Scarecrow, the Tin Man, and the Cowardly Lion, Dorothy articulated the vision to them with a passion and conviction that inspired them to join the team in pursuit of a common objective.

While the end of the journey would yield different benefits for each of them—a way home to Kansas, a brain, a heart, and courage—they had clear objectives of getting to Emerald City and meeting with the Wizard. This sustained them throughout their journey despite the numerous challenges and obstacles they encountered. The same principles apply to a project.

In my youth, one of my managers said to me, "Jim, imagine you are in the building of your biggest client. You are now riding up on the elevator to a meeting with a group of the client's staff members on the 14th floor. On the 11th floor the elevator stops and the door opens. In walks the president of the organization and he presses the 12th-floor button. He looks at you and says, 'Hi, I am the Big Cheese, so tell me what you do around here.' You only have one floor to tell him, or about 10 seconds. What you say in those 10 seconds could change your life for better or worse." This is what is known as the "elevator pitch." You and all your team members should be able to recite the "elevator pitch" or convey the major business objectives of the project in 10 seconds.

A complicated explanation generally denotes a lack of understanding. A clear and concise interpretation of the objectives and concrete deliverables can smooth any project's rough spots and help minimize challenges and obstacles to success. If you can't explain it in 10 seconds, you probably have not got it right.

Point 3: Big Picture

Always look at the big picture.

Today a common practice in many corporations is to have every employee, from the CEO to the entry-level clerk, define their business objectives for the year and make a commitment to achieve them. For example, these may include milestones linked to bonus money. The results are then measured against the committed objectives. The objectives roll down throughout the organization starting at the executive level. This practice ensures that everyone knows and understands the objectives of the corporation and the management chain, and that each set of objectives from the bottom up can be defined to support the objectives of the next level—all the way up to the highest-level corporate objectives. Everyone should understand the big picture, where they fit in, how they can contribute, and how to realize the corporate vision or the big picture.

"Clearly identify the projects and tasks with agreed-upon goals," said David Voran of Cerner. Wing Lee of Sprint added, "Business problems come first, so we need to deliver something quickly." A successful project will share those same characteristics of the roll-up to the big picture. The project objectives must map to the corporate vision or the big picture. You must share these objectives with others and communicate goals and how the goals fit into the big picture with the entire group. You must test the level of understanding and have a checkpoint system to ensure consistencies with the big picture. Insist on "real world" feedback on the feasibility of the project and continually solicit it from the project staff.

Key activities in the planning and requirements phase of any project should be to determine whether the project is achievable within the time frame specified, make sure it is doable for the money being allocated, and verify that the requirements match up with the big picture. Why bother to initiate a project if you can't be relatively assured of its success and that it fits into the big picture? Also, look at your big picture and do not take on the project with inadequate resources or unrealistic time frames. "Achievability" as it relates to the big picture should be continuously monitored throughout the project's life cycle.

Point 4: Speed

There is a need for speed, for time is the enemy of all projects.

"One of the keys to speed is more chaos, less stability," said Tim Chou, former president of Oracle Business Online. For example, an F16 jet is referred to as dynamically unstable. If the active control system should fail, the plane will crash. You build a plane this way because it can turn a lot faster being on the edge of stability. This is a lesson that is very difficult because most of us have grown up in organizations that are stable, and these organizations teach employees lots of ways to create a stable organization. This is antithetical to changing quickly. On the other hand, too much change too quickly can destabilize projects or organizations. Knowing when to push the envelope is a delicate balance.

Another key to speed is more digitization, less talk. Get people out of the loop. Chou gave these examples: In the digitization of banking it costs $1.25 for a teller transaction; a transaction by phone is $.54; a transaction by ATM is $.24, and a transaction over the Internet is $.02. This is a massive change of cost. In another example, Corning digitized its procurement and dropped its cost to purchase parts from $140 to $7. In another study, we saw the cost to process job applications go from more than $100 down to $.06. Oracle did a massive program to do this process. There have been a lot of discussions on the billion dollar savings. Much of these savings are coming from the digitization of sales and support.

Another key to speed is more consolidation, less distribution. The Internet allows you to have one Web site for your corporate information, e-mail, sales literature, and all your business functions. Oracle at one point had more than 200 sites. A change often took months. Now Oracle has a single installation and changes can take minutes.

Another key to speed is more core with less context. Focus on your core business and outsource your business context. Get rid of anything that is not core to the business. For example, for Chuck E. Cheese the pizza is context, whereas for Pizza Hut the pizza is core. Another example is financial systems. You do not get a competitive advantage from building general ledger systems.

Point 5: Yardstick

Projects need measurements to stay on track.

Obviously, there are things beyond anyone's control that can negatively impact a project, but many of these factors can also be mitigated through risk and dependency management. Project objectives need to be clearly stated and defined, and they also need to be measurable. We like stepping-stones—concrete, verifiable, and visible deliverables as measurable items.

To deliver stepping-stones, you need to have the appropriate combination of resources available: people, time, money, and skills. The project plan needs to contain adequate stepping-stones. Each stepping-stone should have a cost, risk, and gain analysis performed. You need to consider identifying and managing possible roadblocks and potholes in your effort to move from stepping-stone to stepping-stone.

Measurements are a barometer to assess a project's status. While often viewed as a necessary evil, they provide a wealth of information and serve a multitude of purposes. Measurements quantify a "gut feeling" of how well or how poorly a project is doing. If undertaken regularly, measurements provide the opportunity for not only ticking off successes, but also allowing for early recognition and correction of problems, justification for resources and funding, and preventive planning on future projects.

Measurements only have value if they are meaningful. That is why Standish Group is against milestones. Milestones are false indicators of progress; they give you an artificial sense of security. You must understand what is being measured, why it is being measured, and if or how it can be measured. Too often measurements take on a life of their own and become projects in and of themselves, rendering them meaningless instead of valuable indicators and tools for communication. Beware of analysis paralysis. You should have a specification for quantity of measurements. You need to have the right tools to capture your measurements. You need to have a methodology to support the measurements with a data collection mechanism. You require the information to support remedial actions. Unless the goals are measurable and verifiable, you may find that what you consider successful, others may consider a failure. "It could just be your definition of success is different from their definition of success," said Julie Deak of John Hancock Insurance.

Point 6: Return on Investment

Return on investment (ROI) is a good place to start when looking at the business objective.

In most commercial businesses there are only two types of project objectives: those mandated by government organizations, such as the IRS, or those done to improve the profits and value of the organization. Projects are made up of features and functions. So concentrating on the scope with regards to return is an interesting concept, since all features and functions will have their own ROI. By understanding the ROI of each feature and function, scope can be changed by priorities for the maximum return to match the business objective. Some functions may have no return and very little impact on the business objective, so why do them at all?

The cost part of the ROI formula starts when the project begins and continues through the cost of ongoing operations and support. In most cases, the return will begin when the project is completed and implemented. There is a way to start the return earlier, however, by looking at the features and functions with the highest return and implementing them first. If the ROI starts early, the project could become healthier. In fact, you may never implement the low ROI features and functions as business needs change and new and more valuable items are identified.

This could also be true for the projects themselves. Projects with higher business value need to be prioritized by their return on investment and business value. The Holy Grail of project management would be to go one step further and view these projects as you would a portfolio of assets. As Gordon Divitt said, "I suggest that a company needs to look at its universe of projects to ensure that it doesn't have too many high-risk ones running at the same time. Just like a stock portfolio, you need to introduce the element of risk and diversity to your portfolio." This is true for individual projects as well as for the features and functions within a project. By measuring the risk/reward ratio at each of your major junctions, you can then start to see a truly useful project.

Point 7: Collaboration

Collaborate with project contributors and stakeholders.

Correctness in translation of what people are saying back and forth plays an extremely important role in what's going on. Establishing clear and concise business objectives is imperative. Collaborating with all project contributors and stakeholders can help you recognize weaknesses and tension points, determine priorities, as well as identify potential setbacks. However, all too often many stakeholders are indifferent or unaware of what the business hopes to achieve and the expected benefits derived through the project.

The race for the resources is measured by answers to some very tough questions. For example, should the organization invest in this project or should it hire more salespeople, open a new plant, or develop a new product? Consensus can occur when you can analyze, learn from, and build upon a combined knowledge base through stakeholder collaboration and feedback. In order to do this you need to create an open environment where honest mistakes or wild ideas are not penalized or criticized.

Collaboration can also foster ownership. Stakeholders are inclined to have a stronger commitment and sense of ownership of the project if they feel their participation and contributions are valued. Through collaboration techniques you can encourage input and feedback from stakeholders to create that sense of ownership. It's also important to celebrate successes, even the little victories. A job well done may be its own reward, but more tangible rewards in the form of money, promotions, or attendance at recognition events can substantially increase commitment from participants.

Third party and outside evaluations can be used to add additional input, sanity checks, and collaboration. For example, in The Standish Group CHAOS database we have ROI numbers with which we can use to profile your project to see if you are within ranges of the average. If your project's projected ROI is higher than average, maybe you are too optimistic, or if your projection is lower than average, maybe you are being too conservative.

By collaborating with stakeholders and third parties you may uncover value you did not originally perceive. All too often we forget that stakeholders are listening to their own songs on that great radio station, WIIFM — What's In It For Me?

Point 8: Peer Review

A strong foundation for a peer review process can greatly benefit projects.

Fewer than 50 percent of organizations today have a formal review process for their projects. When the British government created the Office of Government Commerce (OGC) and set up its peer review system, it discovered the majority of projects did not have a workable plan. The OGC now stops a project until it has a sound business plan and clear objectives. This has saved the British taxpayer billions. A similar process could work in your organization. Peers in various departments could review your business objectives to see if they are clear and comprehensible. Peer reviews also act as another sanity check to foresee any issues or concerns.

Peers often bring to the table their own experiences and can add value to the project. Here is how it might work with a peer review foundation: First, your organization creates a pool of peer reviewers. You might consider outside consultants and advisers as part of your pool. Second, establish a system that specifies which types of projects will be subject to peer reviews, such as projects of a certain size or importance. While some organizations require all projects to undergo a peer review, others determine reviews by a project's scope and type. Third, part of the foundation of peer reviews is timing, so you also need to consider when reviews should take place. The OGC, for example, has six "gates" with peer reviews at each gate. Fourth, peer selection should be random, but with a mechanism to remove conflicts and political elements. You may consider limiting the outside advisers. For example, if your peer review group consists of three people, then you might include only one adviser from the outside.

The next element in your peer review foundation is determining what to do with the peer reviews. Someone has to decide to unconditionally accept the project, accept it with changes, reject it but encourage revision and invite resubmission, or reject it outright. This, of course, should be the executive sponsor and his or her management team. All too often, people confuse technical strategy with business strategy. "A great technology is not going to overcome a terrible business strategy," cautioned Phil Schaadt, former CIO of Bank of America. Peer review is a great tool for ensuring clear and comprehensible business objectives.

Point 9: Too Many Cooks

Too many cooks spoil the broth

In the year 2000, IBM Global Services was losing about $80 million per year in its Business Innovation Services Division, just in integration projects alone. The money was being lost because consultants in the field would come across problems and not know where to turn for a solution. It was not that the field lacked resources; rather, it was the opposite. The field consultants had all kinds of options. What they lacked was a central repository.

The solution was the creation of the Practitioner Support Network. The network comprised all the resources, manuals, databases, service reps, consultants, and engineers. As problems occurred, the consultants would create both a problem identification and a solution path. This became a case. The network of people would collaborate on the solution path to create this case and it was entered into a case-based reasoning database. The next time a consultant encountered the same problem, the system would direct him or her to that case and the accompanying solution.

It should be understood that this was an internal IBM project. Up until the Practitioner Support Network Project, IBM internal projects clearly reflected the old adage, "The cobbler's son is the poorest shod." The track record for internal IBM projects was dismal and no one we talked to could recount a single success. IBM is so large and diverse, that many stakeholders want input into the projects. This causes scope creep and delays. So for the Practitioner Support Network, IBM decided to try a small development team with a smaller representative group of stakeholders. It had its first release of the Practitioner Support Network implemented within six months and an immediate return on investment.

Point 10: Homework

Always do thorough research for every project.

Many times what seems clear to you is confusing to others. You need to test your theories to make sure the business objectives are understood. You can do this through research. Focus groups are wonderful tools and provide an opportunity for both collaboration and conflict feedback. The best way to run a focus group is to hire a professional moderator and rent a focus group facility. If you end up doing a lot of them you may want to develop the expertise in-house. The following example used focus groups heavily.

In the mid-70s, 10 years before the formation of The Standish Group, two individuals, later to be Standish associates, interviewed executive management from the Commonwealth of Massachusetts' Department of Employment Security (DES) on how their clients used their services. They learned from these interviews that executives wanted to reduce the number of clients they served. The associates then interviewed a number of companies that funded the DES and asked them how DES could be of better service to them. They said that they would like DES to help them find qualified workers. The picture was becoming clear and they could see both sides of equation. Now they needed a plan and a way to present a clear business objective to couple with the problem.

From the information obtained from these two interviewed groups, the team created what we would now call a focus group guide. They went to the local field offices, recruited participants, and conducted a number of focus group sessions with the unemployed workers. They learned from the unemployed workers through the focus groups how they would like DES to help them find work. Using information from these focus groups, they then constructed a survey instrument and executed a broad-based survey. The survey tested the business objectives and different ways workers could access jobs. The two to-be Standish associates then went back to the DES executive and proposed a database of available jobs to be run by DES. The result was the creation of the first JobBank, a searchable database of open job opportunities. This all came about through research, and the key findings were obtained from the focus groups and surveys.

In Conclusion

Meeting and beating the competition is a frequent business objective, but it must be quantifiable. If one bank offers online banking, other banks need to offer it as well — even though they may not be able to justify the project from a return on investment standpoint. If the bank can keep a customer from going to its competitor, what does this do to the bottom line? What if the customer would have left anyway? How much does it cost to gain new customers? Measuring the value of anything is difficult; therefore, clear business objectives are a must as the first step in measuring the value of a project.

This lesson on clear business objectives covered the following points: Point 1 discussed the necessity of getting everyone on the same page. You must make sure everyone has the same understanding of the project's business objectives. Point 2, the "elevator pitch," talked about making the business objectives concise and comprehensible. Stakeholders should be able to present the project in 10 seconds or less. Point 3 stressed the big picture and knowing how the project fits into the overall organization's strategy. Point 4 covered speed and how the clarity of business objectives can increase speed. Point 5 talked about using a yardstick to measure project progress. Point 6 considered return on investment (ROI) as a clear business objective. Point 7 reflected on collaboration as a way to ensure a clear and concise message on business objectives. Point 8 described a foundation for peer review and the accompanying benefits. Point 9 illustrated how having too many stakeholders can spoil the project. Point 10 covered the importance of conducting basic and fundamental research.

User involvement, executive support, and clear business objectives are the big three in the list of CHAOS Success Factors. In Standish Group's risk measurement system, these factors account for 50 percent of the grade. Therefore, doing these three things well will get you halfway to a successful project. The following lessons detail the additional CHAOS Success Factors, which play a supporting role to these big three.

Lesson Four: The Great Molasses Flood

It had been cold for several days. Boston's daily temperature was averaging nearly zero degrees Fahrenheit. Then, on January 15, 1919, the noontime temperature reached 40 degrees. Standing over 50 feet tall and holding 2.5 million gallons of sweet brown molasses, The Purity Distilling Co.'s molasses tank could hold no more. The sudden rise in temperature caused the molasses to expand and the tank exploded. A 30-foot-high molasses tsunami, traveling at 30 miles per hour, flooded Commercial Street and other nearby Boston streets. The Great Molasses Flood killed 21 people and injured 150 others.

The wave also destroyed millions of dollars worth of property. Part of Boston's elevated train line was destroyed. Trapped horses had to be shot. It took more than six months to remove the molasses from the cobblestone streets. To this day, many Bostonians claim they can still smell traces of molasses on a hot summer day.

Like the molasses tank, the expansion of requirements can cause a project disaster. In the beginning of a project, the key to reducing both time and money is constraining scope to just those elements that are absolutely necessary. This is optimal. As you move forward you look at cost, risk, and gain of each requirement to optimize your scope. Scope is a collection of requirements. Scope equals time, and time equals money. Time is the enemy of all projects, and money is the root of all evil! And molasses, oddly enough, can kill.

Point 1: Scope

The scope of a project must be contained.

The natural expectation is for project stakeholders to want it all, thus enlarging project scope. "We call this boiling the ocean, where everybody decides that a data warehouse is the single repository of every fact known since the beginning of mankind," said David Kirk of America Online. Determining how much can be accomplished realistically in the available time frame always presents a challenge.

"The three things that caused us to go over budget were scope creep, scope creep, and more scope creep," said Mike Manis of Harrah's Entertainment. Managing scope is a never-ending task and frequent, open review of it is a must. That means presenting a view of, "Here is where we are, here is where we are going, and this is what is happening with the scope of the project." Do that often.

It's unlikely you'd build a house with no objective in mind other than to have some place to sleep. You need to know how many floors you want, the number rooms, and the square footage. Software projects work the same way. First, the project should have a top-down design and you must understand the scope of the "big picture." You need to divide the project into chewable chunks or manageable pieces that add up to the overall scope, just like you would in building a house. Each piece of the project should have a concrete deliverable, foundation, framing, and so on. These need to be broken down to the optimal level, such as pouring the concrete foundation before starting the framing. You need to remove as many interdependencies as possible and constantly monitor the rest.

Through many research projects, Standish Group has found that fewer than 20 percent of software features actually get used. The following steps may help you in managing scope: Have a benefit statement for each feature and function, including cost, ROI, and risk. Each feature and function should be given a priority based against the other features and functions. A real danger signal is when the executive sponsor or other stakeholders say they must have it all or the system is no good to them. This is just not a reality, and such a proclamation is not a requirement, but a death sentence.

Point 2: Stepping-stones

There is a difference between stepping-stones and milestones. Projects should use stepping-stones.

The Standish Group has said for many years that establishing small project milestones is an insurance policy that mitigates the risk of committing an unrecoverable error in a project. However, we now believe that milestones, whether small or large, are just plain bad. In a project group therapy session a few years ago, we asked one of the delegates how far the project got with the previous effort and the reply was, "We got to about 90 percent completion." Astonished by this revelation, we followed up with the obvious question, "Then why did you cancel the project?" The retort was, "Because we had 90 percent left to go!"

Standish Group suggests you need break up a project into small stepping-stones. A stepping-stone is like a milestone, but it is a firm deliverable. Stepping-stones allow you to track progress based on these firm deliverables. The traditional project management way has been to track progress based on milestones. Now, milestones can work fine for a trip in your car where you know how far you are going, but projects don't work that way. In tracking software project requirements, milestone can be misleading and they are false indicators of progress — they are false metrics. Stepping-stones allow you to see the output and test to make sure it does what you are expecting it to do. If it doesn't work, you can throw it away and back up to the last good stepping-stone and try a different path. Prototyping is a good tool for creating stepping-stones.

On the other hand, the content of the milestones must be objectively defined and well understood. Second, milestones must be measurable and quantifiable; this process is often arbitrary and error-prone. It is very difficult to create the level of granularity by which milestones are set. They can be influenced by many factors. "We want to move the current application to a new platform. This has been a time box problem," said Robert Gibson of Visiting Nurse Health System. The impact of missing the milestone on the success or failure of a project can elevate it to high visibility, mandating frequent monitoring that will cause more overhead tracking false metrics.

Stepping-stones are easy because you can see them. Each stepping-stone is assigned an owner who is responsible and accountable for its completion. Your project plan should comprise identifiable stepping-stones that are measurable, quantifiable, and concrete.

Point 3: Time Boxing

Consider the use of time boxing, which involves set deadlines and a fixed amount of time in which to complete the project or stepping-stones.

Extreme Programming recommends a week to complete a requirement depicted on a 3x5 index card, although some organizations use a two-week time box. With the Scrum method, it is a month. "In reality these things are always changing and the discovery phase is an ongoing process," said Greg Cherry of Acxion. You should consider the use of time boxing and a prioritized feature list. First, estimate the resources required to complete the project by each requirement. Then make sure you have the availability of the required resources for each of these requirements. Then you can set your time boxes in motion.

It has been said that proper prior planning prevents problems — the five Ps of project management (PM). The moment to establish project stepping-stones with time boxes is at the beginning of the project or in the planning phase. It's important to take the time to consider the 80/20 rule as it applies to projects: 80 percent of the user benefits will be derived from 20 percent of a project's features. If you do not know your stakeholders' true needs, you cannot provide them with solutions. A good rule for success is having a modest baseline. In most cases baseline requirements are items that must be present or the system just will not work. A modest baseline is when you understand your bare minimum requirements and get all the stakeholders' approval for these. Then you can time box each requirement.

After the baseline is completed, you can move on to other requirements. Each of these requirements should also be time boxed. Do the most important items with the least risk first, and start going down the list in the same manner. Save the low-value, high-risk items until the end, or even better, do not do them at all. Time is the enemy of all projects, and money is the root of all evil. The key to reducing both time and money is constraining scope to just those things that are necessary.

Point 4: Rules

Rules give you a clear idea of a project's priorities, and how you know you are doing the right things.

You need to know the most important features within a project. You also must know which project needs to be worked on next week. And you need to have a clear idea of your strategy and how your technology impacts that strategy. Companies are trying to learn how to execute technology decisions and deliverables more efficiently. Everyone wants to streamline the business process. It has become mission-critical. This impact creates significant challenges for those responsible for building new products and maintaining the existing infrastructure. Therefore, coordinating the teams, tools, and techniques involved in any project is absolutely imperative. In order to do this, you need rules of engagement.

A successful program requires the clear articulation of important rules, such as what activities are necessary, how they should be performed, and what resources are needed. Therefore, rules serve as the fundamental tools of any project, especially to align the IT objective with the overall business goals and strategies.

Rules are uncomplicated tools that control the flow of the project features and functions. A rule, for example, might state that no feature can be implemented with an ROI of less than 10 percent. Rules are critical to environments with multiple projects that share distributed development information. First and foremost, an effective project implementation requires a cogent project plan that encompasses the procedures, guidelines, techniques, tools, project templates, and rules. All contributors must understand the rules and how they relate to the organization's requirements.

Figuring out how you can link your strategy to your technology decisions is instrumental to maintaining an organized development environment throughout the duration of any project. Business takes place in a relationship and everyone needs to know the rules of engagement. Keeping this in mind can make or break a project. It takes coordination and cooperation of the people, processes, and products to carry out a project. Rules provide the platform for cooperation. Keeping the entire project group informed about the rules empowers and educates the team and management alike. Rules help to eliminate inconsistency and misinformation that can promote uncertainty. Rules can help you optimize the scope.

Point 5: Expectations

Managing expectations is crucial.

By minimizing and optimizing the scope, it is much easier to set expectations. Remember the saying, "If you don't expect much, you will never be disappointed." Dennis Nash of U.S. Internetworking put it a different way: "The delta between reality and expectations is disappointment." On the other hand, some people never learn. "Being the idiots that we were, we agreed to it," said Martin Edelman of Creative System Software, referring to a project. Losing control of scope is often the first step on the road to projects that come in over budget, are late, do not meet specifications, or are canceled.

In the early 1990s, a start-up company landed its first contract from the South Korean government for a census and vital statistic system. The fee to build the system was $12 million. The first thing the company learned was that the client did not know what it wanted. The second lesson was that the people who would do the actual work did not speak English, and project manager Jim Olivera and his team knew no Korean. But as Olivera said: "We were young and stupid. We thought we could conquer the world; they wanted the world and we were ready to give it to them."

After months of changes and added scope, the project was failing. One night during a heavy dinner of food and drink, Mr. Lee, the Korean governmentt executive in charge of the project turned to Olivera and asked if the project would be successful. Olivera replied: "Absolutely. I guarantee it, Mr. Lee". At that, Mr. Lee asked for Olivera's passport and told him if the project was not successful he, Mr. Lee, would have to commit suicide, because he would lose face. Mr. Lee also relayed that a guarantee means that you will do everything in your power to make the project successful, including divorcing your wife, leaving your kids, and moving to Korea.

Olivera did not divorce his wife or leave his kids. He did, however, move to Korea for the next year and a half and the application did get completed, at a much higher cost to the new company, which lead to the start-up's demise.

Point 6: Index Cards

You can optimize scope through the use of a small medium, like an index card.

Blaise Pascal once wrote: "I made this letter longer than usual because I lack the time to make it short." Condensing a thought is often harder work than expanding it.

In the Extreme Programming method, there are interesting practices centered on the notion of conversation. Requirements and specifications are put down on 3X5 or 5X8 inch index cards. The collection of cards is a story, with each card being one part of the story. Users, or more often business analysts, do the writing based on user inputs on the story cards, and developers have conversations with the users about them. Developers write code to each story card, with each card equaling approximately one week of work. Developers work in pairs and have conversations about the story cards. When a story card is finished it is checked for quality (the tests are actually written before the code) and presented to the user. Users then have conversations with the developers about the finished code. It's Friday and the week has ended.

On Monday morning the users have conversations with developers on the next story card. If there has been a change in priority, then the cards are swapped, not shuffled. Since each card should represent a week of work, programming time should be much easier to estimate. For example, if the project needs to be completed in 12 weeks and there are 16 cards, then four cards would need to be dropped. Also, if one card ends up taking two weeks instead of one week, then the date would have to be changed.

Kent Beck, the father of Extreme Programming, proposes "conversation" as the paradigm, and suggests using index cards as a means to create dialog between business and technology. Extreme Programming is one example of agile development methods, which rely on small media to help reduce scope. Optimizing scope can go a long way toward achieving project success. They truly fit into what Standish has learned from our body of research. After all, everybody knows what happens when you try fit 10 pounds of potatoes into a 5-pound bag.

Point 7: Role Models

Look to role models for guidance, both good and bad.

It is rare that we can present projects that are truly identical, but the U.S. federal government provided 50 of them. Here we present the best and the worst. The initiatives surrounding the implementation of the Statewide Automated Child Welfare Information Systems (SACWIS) began with the best of intentions and this premise. Congress made amendments to the Social Security Act in 1986 requiring statewide data reporting systems to better evaluate countrywide child welfare issues.

Florida's work on this project began in 1990 with a plan for completion in 1998. The original cost estimate was $32 million. The final cost was more than $230 million and it went live the summer of 2005. The state had 109 people on the project team. As if this weren't bad enough, the state paid for three IBM consultants to run the project. These consultants were responsible for performing the following three jobs: project manager, project architect, and project analyst! Just the salary alone for these three people was budgeted at $1.8 million per year.

In contrast, the State of Minnesota began its SACWIS project in 1999 with eight people. They concentrated on creating a standard infrastructure for collecting data and relied heavily on user involvement to minimize requirements and focus on the essential ones. They used no consultants, but instead found vendors that would partner with them when additional skills were required. Phase One was completed in seven months and Phase Two was completed by mid-year 2000. The state spent $1.1 million.

The SACWIS Project goal was aimed at serving the needs of children. The basic requirement was to access accurate and detailed information related to cases more easily, and in a timely manner. While the requirements for what was to be included in a SACWIS system were vague and largely open to interpretation, the overall goal was to deliver a single, integrated system for the recording and collection of child protective, preventive, foster care, and adoption service information, statewide. The State of Florida created a much larger scope and spent 230 percent more than the State of Minnesota, which optimized its requirements. I know which role model I would consider.

Point 8: Yield

Assess project requirements by their yield or gain.

For many years the IT industry has categorized requirements into three buckets: mandatory, must have, and nice to have. I would like to consider a different categorization: baseline, yield, and non-yield. A baseline is a requirement that, without it, the system will simply not work. Examples of this type of function might be database access or the ability to read a credit card. Yield requirements are items for which an ROI number or a value can be assessed. Non-yield requirements are not baseline items, nor can they show a return or value.

The assessment process is iterative and dynamic. First, working with your stakeholders, start with an ROI or value for the project. Remember a reasonable estimate is a key ingredient to an accurate ROI. You then take each requirement and put it into one of the three categories. Calculate an ROI on each of the "yield" features and functions, and add up all the yield numbers. Subtract this figure from the overall ROI. That is your baseline ROI. If you come out with a negative number you have done something wrong; you will need to go back and reassess your overall ROI and the yield requirements.

You can start the project by completing the baseline requirements. Once the baseline is complete, you can implement the system or wait until some of the yield items are functional. Next, work on the high-yield items first and make your way down the list. As each requirement is completed, you and the stakeholders must reassess the ROI and priority of the remaining ones. Implementing requirements that support the current business case as rapidly as possible is a key to maximizing ROI and gaining feedback on feature relevance. The quicker the implementation, the greater the yield. Non-yield functions need to be considered on a case-by-case basis. Project ROI can be a moving target and should not be a one-time or static event. It should follow the life cycle of the system.

Point 9: Risk

Consider the risk of each requirement.

Requirements in the context of project management are groups of tasks that build, develop, and implement software components, objects, and code. You have by now put requirements into three different categories: baseline, yield, and non-yield. Like tying the ROI to requirements, tying risk to this process is also a very iterative and dynamic process. First, every project has risk, so you should start with a risk assessment. This can be easy or hard. It is easy if you ask The Standish Group. We will give you your project's overall probability of success. If the risk of failure is too great, you should weigh an alternative path or consider reducing the complexity, as well as the risky behavior.

Here is one process you can use for reducing the complexity. From your ROI, you already have taken each requirement and put it into the three categories. Now assign each requirement a complexity number from 1 to 10, with 10 being the highest. Remember complexity causes confusion and expense, or increased risk. If the baseline requirements all have high numbers, you should consider the project at higher risk; lower numbers indicate a lower risk.

As you decide to go forward, start the project by working on the baseline first. Once the baseline is completed you can implement the system or wait until some of the other items are functional. You, and your stakeholders, have already ranked the requirements by the cost and ROI, so now you can reorder the requirements by risk and reward. Start with the high-yield and the lowest-risk items first and work down the list. Work with the stakeholders to try to eliminate low-yield and high-risk requirements.

The three elements that you need to consider for each requirement are cost, risk, and gain. By just focusing on these three elements can greatly clarify your project and ensure that you are moving in the right direction.

Chart 10

What is your general process for optimizing requirements?
(Pick the one closest to your method)

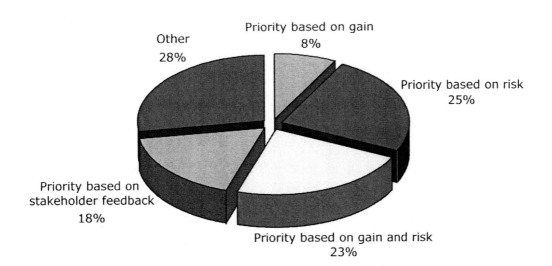

Source: DARTS January 2006

Point 10: Panda Bears

Sometimes you keep the panda bear; sometimes you don't.

  Consider cost, risk, and gain collectively in your decision-making. To test our theory and find out how it might work, we conducted three workshops at one of our CHAOS University events and followed it up with several other events. At each event the group broke into groups of five to 10 participants. We set up a program to build a zoo called Cat Mountain Zoo. Cat Mountain Zoo had five exhibit projects, such as a bird aviary. Each of the exhibit projects had five requirements; for example, the monkey compound project had accommodations for chimpanzees, baboons, spider monkeys, gorillas, and lemurs. The Bear River exhibit included a panda bear.

  Every requirement was assigned a cost, a return rate, a net gain, a risk percent, and the amount of money at risk. There are a few ways to calculate money at risk. In our workshop, we used the project cost, added the average overrun, and multiplied by the percent of risk. The total cost of the program was $5 million. In the first workshop the participants' task was to reduce the cost to $4 million while maximizing the net gain. One person from each of the groups was given a project; the remaining participants were users. For the most part, the groups accomplished the first task fairly easily. For example, every group kept the panda bear, which had the highest return rate and a solid net gain.

  In the second workshop, the task was to reduce the money at risk while cutting the budget to $4 million dollars. The risk had to be cut from almost $2 million to $1 million. Again, the groups worked hard and, after some negotiating, got their risk down to under a million. It should be noted that the first animal to go was the panda bear, which also had the highest risk.

  In the third workshop, the task was to maximize the return and minimize the risk. This proved to be a most daunting task. The panda bear turn out to be a pivotal decision since it represented the highest cost, risk, and gain. Those who could tolerate higher risk kept the panda bear, while others sent it back to China. As the teams worked, they realized in order to optimize your requirements you must look at the aspects of cost, risk, and gain.

In Conclusion

Optimizing scope minimizes risk and maximizes return. Members of the IT community must remember that the only reason a project exists is to satisfy the needs of the user community and, ultimately, to benefit an organization. To optimize scope, focus on the true needs and benefits.

In this lesson on optimizing scope, Point 1 talked about minimizing scope to facilitate optimization. Point 2 discussed the merits of stepping-stones and the dangers of milestones. Time is the enemy of all projects, and if you can box them in you can achieve success. Point 3 covered the use of time boxing, which involves set deadlines and a fixed amount of time in which to complete the project or stepping-stones. Point 4 looked at rules of engagement. Point 5 discussed managing expectations by minimizing and optimizing the scope.

The use of a small medium like index cards to help optimize scope was the focus of Point 6. Point 7 illustrated how the use of role models can be a guide for both good and bad behavior. Point 8 covered assessing the need of a requirement by its yield or gain. Point 9 considered the risk requirements. The last point considered cost, risk, and gain in tandem as elements for optimizing scope.

Finally, projects must be continuously reevaluated in terms of their meaning to the future of the business. In order to determine whether or not you have optimized scope for a particular project, consider these last items: The optimal scope must be consistent with the business strategy. You must break down the scope into short-term, mid-term, and long-term objectives and communicate these objectives to all the stakeholders. The scope of a project should have buy-in from the stakeholders, and there should be a procedure for constant reevaluation. Comedian Bill Cosby once said: "I don't know the key to success, but the key to failure is to try to please everyone."

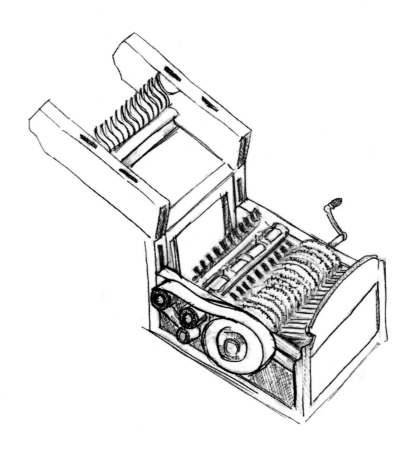

Lesson Five: Cotton Gin

The cotton that grew inland in the southern United States had tacky green seeds that took workers several hours to remove from the fluffy white plants. Southern planters were discouraged because profits were short and labor was long. In 1793, Eli Whitney invented the cotton gin. Whitney's invention suddenly made growing cotton very profitable, and cotton production skyrocketed over the next five decades. Although Whitney patented his invention through the U.S. Patent Office, it did not make him rich. Many of the farmers either worked around his patent or ignored it altogether.

Whitney grew rich from his lesser-known invention — mass production. He devised a way to make standard parts through machines, thus making them interchangeable. A prime example of the use of his invention was the Model T Ford. By 1913, the Model T was being mass- produced by a rolling assembly line with three basic manufacturing concepts, interchangeable parts, continuous flow, and specialized jobs. The heart of it was the notion that each worker had a particular activity and did their assignments over and over again. Henry Ford divided the tasks into eighty-four discrete steps. Prior to Ford, each car was one-of-kind and built on a rail by an expert team that could do every task in the assembly and manufacturing of an automobile. By off-railing the parts and tasks, Ford increased production and reduced cost to where the factory workers could afford to by one of Ford's new automobiles.

These are the basic concepts of the agile process. Develop interchangeable objects in a continuous flow by specialized teams. There are no easy answers to the development of software. There is no panacea. It is just a lot of hard work. The old joke asks, "How do you eat an elephant?" The answer is: "One bite at a time!" That is the agile process, building software one bite at a time.

Point 1: Iterative

Project success requires an iterative development style.

Standish Group's CHAOS research clearly shows that the smaller the project, the greater the success rate. The iterative development style is the ultimate in small projects. Basically, iterative development consists of a series of tiny projects. In the early '90s Standish Group published the iterative development process; since then, iterative has become the basic foundation of multiple agile types of methodologies, such as Extreme Programming (XP), Scrum, or Rational Unified Process (RUP). The iterative process has five basic components: baseline, requirements, development, testing, and deployment.

Once you have decided to go forward with a project and you are going to use an agile method, the baseline is the beginning of the process, or step zero. After the baseline has gone through the requirements, development, testing, and deployment steps, then you circle back to the requirements, development, testing, and deployment steps and again and again.

The first step in any agile process is requirements. In the requirements phase, you need to make sure that anything being developed is absolutely necessary for the basic system to work. It is not about the vision; it is about necessity.

If you are using XP, you will have to write "stories" and the stories are broken down into a week's worth of work on index cards. You then pick the next index card or cards to work on.

The second step is development. Again, in the case of XP, this represents a week's worth of work done by pairs of programmers, in collaboration with a user to help clarify and provide rapid feedback. If you find that this does not meet the user's needs, you scrap the code and go back to step one.

The third step is testing and quality control. In the XP model the testing needs are written on the other side of the index card. Automatic testing and inspection can speed the process along and build an iterative testing suite. Of course, the ultimate testing is in the user's hand.

The last step is deployment. Once the new code has been written, tested, and signed off by the users, it is now ready for use. If this is not the end of the project, you go back to step one. Otherwise, you claim victory and move on to your next project.

Point 2: Collaboration

Collaboration is key to the agile development process.

Understanding that communication is the most crucial aspect of a project is the core of collaborative management. While the project manager remains chief project intermediary, individual project stakeholders, from sponsor to developer, are vital to the project outcome in their own right. Project management has always been a team-oriented venture headed by a project manager or leader; however, the role of the project manager as chief coordinator and communicator has diminished. Now, the focus is on even distribution and dissemination of project-specific knowledge to every project contributor. After all, projects require group effort as much as individual contribution. Crazy Horse could not have won the Battle of Little Big Horn alone.

The Web is now the most common business medium and it is a standard software infrastructure. It is boundless, without time barriers. It fits perfectly into the agile development process. Changes, additions, and corrections can be implemented in real time or close to real time. This is a key point, because it drives one of the cornerstones of the agile process: trial and error.

While requirements documents and use cases go a long way toward providing basic specifications, it is sometimes impossible to capture the user's true meaning. Many, if not most, automation systems include the user performing some manual tasks that could be automated. In this case, for example, the developer would create a function to automate the manual task and allow the user to test and use it. The stakeholders provide immediate feedback to the developer. In the case of XP, the users are with the developers, while in Scrum the feedback occurs after a sprint, or 30 days of work. If the user accepts the function, the developer moves on to the next function; if not, the developer tries again. In order for this collaborative process to work, it must be simple and quick, without a lot of fanfare.

The user could be any place and, therefore, Web-based collaboration tools like WebEx are very helpful. The developer can show the users functionality prior to test or implementation. In fact, the users should not have to move from their offices to test and use the new function.

Point 3: Rapid Feedback

Quickness and velocity are vital to an agile process, and that encompasses feedback. It should be rapid.

It is a fact of life that you can only digest small bits of information at one time. This fits perfectly into the agile process. In order to do this you must set up a structure that everyone understands and is easily implemented, and that only looks at small accomplishments such as stepping-stones. You want to get feedback on a regular basis through frequent reviews, such as with Scrum. In the case of XP, users are embedded into the development teams.

Poorly accepted feedback can undermine velocity and cause delays. You must create and maintain an environment in which stakeholders feel comfortable in providing feedback quickly and easily. People generally improve their feedback when they receive candid, fair, and timely responses to their comments and suggestions. Stakeholders need to give feedback on a timely basis, such as when critical stepping-stones have been built; developers need those comments before moving on to other stepping-stones. Accuracy is another issue; the feedback needs to be monitored to prevent or mitigate mistakes or misdirection. Prepared feedback and response forms can help prevent mistakes and improve rapid response.

Another way to prevent mistakes is to not only provide your response to the feedback, but also provide feedback on the stakeholders' feedback. This should be given in only the most positive manner. For example, you may say to the user, "It would be helpful to us if you could provide an example of that situation." Another method is the use of surveys and focus groups to discover how stakeholders perceive the project's progress and results. You can also use the Web to conduct surveys and forums. WebEx is a good tool to demonstrate prototypes and new features, functions, and ideas. This format provides the most rapid feedback, which is real time. You could also use WebEx for real-time focus groups. Standish Group has been conducting focus groups for years over WebEx, and we have found it to be a wonderful tool. Time is the enemy of all projects, and rapid feedback reduces time. However, you need to structure the project to promote and accept rapid feedback.

Chart 11

Percent of Applications Outage Events by Cause

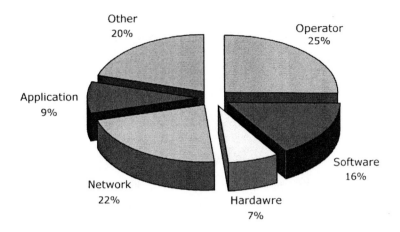

Percent of Applications Outage Time by Cause

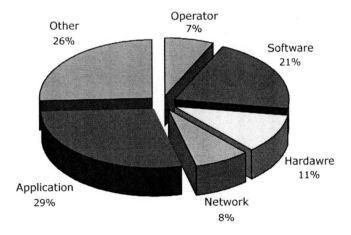

Source: CENTS January 2005 to December 2005

Point 4: Quality

Test code quality early and often.

Standish Group's research shows that coding errors and programming bugs cause the vast majority of all application outages, well above hardware, network, and database failures. On the other hand, quality assurance is frequently the first area that is cut back when deadlines are missed. This, of course, increases the problem. An error caught within the development process is from 10 to 100 times cheaper to correct than a bug found during the application's operation.

Building the testing suites and data prior to building the code can help in many ways. According to Extreme Programming advocates, the combined time it takes to create a unit test, and create some code to make it pass, is about the same as just coding it. By building the test prior to coding you save time and a lot of heartache.

Constructing testing scenarios and making them part of the specification is also a good way to make sure your code matches the requirements. The testing and inspection process calls for frequent and rapid testing versus waiting until the end of the development cycle. You should create a toolkit of inspection software and procedures. A developer can run a code testing and inspection process against the newly created code at any time. The test could be run at the end of each day or at the end of the completion of a function. This is almost like spell checking a document. This simple procedure will catch many common errors and ensure compliance with both general and company-specific standards.

The bottom line to a successful quality process is: Do the work and get dirty. Proper planning, maintenance, resources, and a lot of effort will mean the difference between success and failure. It is necessary to be aware of the investment involved in the quality and testing process, and not to be discouraged when the return on investment in terms of dollars is not immediate. The ultimate return will be better software quality. Concentrate on the mechanics of the quality and testing process, and the returns — both tangible and intangible — will follow.

Point 5: Standard Infrastructure

When choosing a standard infrastructure, consider first what business medium will be the most cost-effective for your organization, especially if it interfaces with external customers.

The Web, for example, is the perfect business medium for the base of a standard software infrastructure. It is boundless, and there are no time barriers. Changes, additions, and corrections can be implemented in real time or close to real time. For example, a user asked if we could display the cost and performance inputs as part of the basic output results in the VirtualADVISOR cost assessment model, which is Standish Group's Total Cost of Ownership tool. We were able to turn it around in one day and have it running on the application the next morning — without deploying new client software. While this was a minor change, it demonstrates the power of using the Internet as a standard delivery infrastructure.

Second, choose a server, operating system, and database that will be used for all your major applications, or have rules on what products will be used when and where. This way the developers and management do not have to revisit this issue for every project. It also keeps training to a minimum and makes skills inventory easier to track. This does not mean you have to choose the most popular products; rather, choose products that best suit your business and IT style. However, in developing on these platforms, it is important to stay away from their proprietary extensions that lock you into their technologies.

The third leg of the standard software infrastructure is the middleware toolkit. This is one of the most difficult choices to make, since not all middleware provides the same functionality. Middleware is a toolkit because it offers developers shortcuts for doing customizations. The toolkit provides a way to tailor a range of products that offer needed functionality, such as Web management, security, high availability, message transport, and transaction processing in the way that best fits each application's needs.

It is not necessary to suddenly change your whole IT environment to adopt the standard infrastructure philosophy as part of your agile process, but you should carve out a set of applications to pilot the use of these methods and, as they prove their worth, extend them to more and more projects.

Point 6: No Releases

If release methods are engrained in your software life cycle, break the cycle. No more releases.

The issue of releases is one of the more controversial subjects in this book. New releases are a big part of the software industry. Issuing new releases is how many software companies make money, but for corporate developers, they are just not necessary. Releases are costly, and they usually cause poor quality. They also stifle progress. Some of the most progressive companies, such as WebEx Communications, eBay, and Google, have a no-new-release policy. As the first user of WebEx, I acknowledge it took a bit of getting used to. New functionality would just appear. The nice thing was that new functionality arrived in small doses, so I did not need to learn a lot of new features at one time.

Seeing how WebEx develops and releases software, Standish Group decided to adapt WebEx's method to our development organization. I would never go back to the old way. It does require a change in thinking, and you do need to have a few things in place. First, you need that standard Web-based infrastructure. Second, you need to have and use quality control tools or send the code out overnight to a company like Reasoning Inc. in Sunnyvale, Calif., which offers automated software inspection services. Third, you certainly need change management software to keep track of versions. We would never suggest doing away with versions. Fourth, you need to have an iterative development methodology. Fifth, you need to have a release baseline.

This is how it works. You develop the function over the current code. You test as best as you can within your budget. You add it to the application. If you have done a poor job, you might receive a bunch of calls, but then you fix it. You will know better the next time to do more testing first. However, the big advantage of this approach versus doing releases is you will know right where the problem lies. The other nice thing about this method is there is no patch management—you just fix the problem and forget it. The benefit to no releases is multifold: The process is cheaper, faster, and higher quality; the code is easier to fix and distribute; and educating users is easier.

Point 7: Extreme, RUP, and Scrum

If your software development practices and methodologies are dysfunctional, blame it on Fred. Then get Extreme, RUP, or Scrum.

Kent Beck, author of Extreme Programming Explained (Addison-Wesley Professional, 1999), explained how many of the dysfunctional patterns of software development can be traced directly back to Fred W. Taylor (1856-1915), inventor of Scientific Management. In Beck's talk at CHAOS University titled "Fred Taylor, Making Conversation and Software," he said he believes software development is a lot like the old-style manufacturing process and his Extreme Programming methods break that process.

There are basically four parts to Extreme Programming. They are planning, designing, coding, and testing. Unlike other methodologies, these are not phases; rather, they work in tandem with each other. Planning includes user stories, stand-up meetings, and small releases. The design segment also stresses to not add functionality until it is needed. In the coding part, the user is always available for feedback, developers work in pairs, and the code is written to an agreed standard. In testing, the tests are written before the code.

The Rational Unified Process (RUP) of agile software development methodology, created by Rational Software, now part of IBM, breaks down the development of software into four gates. Each gate consists of iterations of the software at that gate in development. A project stays in a gate until the stakeholders are satisfied, and then it either moves to the next gate or is canceled. Gate one is called the inception of the business case. Gate two, called elaboration, provides a rough order of magnitude. Gate three is called construction, and this where you build the product. Gate four is the transition, or another word for deployment. In this gate you fine-tune the performance, make any final adjustments, educate the users, and install the product. Of course, the user could reject the product and send you back to gate one.

In rugby, a "scrum" is a team pack and everyone in the pack works together to move the ball down the field. It is also the name given to a project management methodology. In the Scrum project methodology, the project team is broken up into smaller teams, each with an appointed goal to achieve. The process of reaching the goal is referred to as a "sprint." A sprint lasts 30 days, with each day ending, or beginning, with a stand-up meeting.

Point 8: Geeks Are Easy

The agile process makes it easy for geeks and users.

"Geeks are easy. Give them more toys, don't yell at them, and they will be happy," said Kent Beck, father of Extreme Programming. Beck, in his talk at CHAOS University, pointed out that Fred W. Taylor's Scientific Management was the platform for the Industrial Revolution. His theories—otherwise known as "Taylorisms"—set the rules for mass production long before Henry Ford started building the Model T. Taylor's four principles of Scientific Management were: 1) workers are financially motivated; 2) there is a proper fit between the worker and the job; 3) there is a difference between management and workers (workers are lazy and stupid); and 4) there is a best way to do a job. Beck quoted Taylor as saying, "In the past man was first; in the future the system will be first." However, IT people are not lazy and stupid. Workers are paid well, but they need more complex motivations; and there is not always "one" best way.

If I had to categorize the three most popular agile process methodologies by management style, Extreme Programming would be socially centric, Scrum would be engineering centric, and RUP would be tool and management centric. In Extreme Programming the users are part of team. The Scrum methodology implies that continual meetings with the users, sponsors, and others disrupt progress for the team and cause delays. Scrum's 30-day sprint only takes place after the users sign off on the specifications. And with RUP it is more about how the tools get used in each gate.

With the Scrum methodology, if the users have a change of heart after the sprint starts, it is more efficient to stop work and go back to the drawing board and get a new set of requirements rather than try to adjust on-the-fly. While with Extreme Programming, the users, who are looking over the developer's shoulder, should be telling him or her what they like or don't like. This ad hoc change of spec could cause scope creep, and having users pitch in random requirements at any time is often a sure recipe for failure. The Scrum process works well when the users are more distant and casual in their use of a product, such as a Web service, and software engineering is central to the outcome. Extreme works best in environments where the users are closer to the application and are uncertain of their true needs. And with RUP is more for IT management that demand exceptional control.

Point 9: Da Vinci Code

Knowing how to give and receive feedback can make or break a project.

In Michael J. Gelb's book, Work Like Da Vinci: Gaining the Creative Advantage in Your Business and Career (Your Coach in a Box) [Coach Series, 2006], he presents what he believes are Da Vinci's seven principles: 1) ask the right questions; 2) put your answers to work; 3) develop your business senses; 4) turn uncertainty into opportunity; 5) strike a profitable balance; 6) integrate for success; and 7) make the breakthrough connection Rapid feedback is a very important part of any project and is especially important to the agile process. Gelb uses the acronym SMART to lay out the principles on giving and receiving good feedback.

The "S" stands for specific. Gelb says that in order for feedback to be effective it must point at particular behavior. Just telling someone he is a slob does little good. Telling someone he should pick up his dirty socks on the floor is an action that person can consider. This, of course, would never work on a teenager and you need to avoid being judgmental.

The "M" is to monitor. If you tell the teenager to pick up his dirty socks and you come back two hours later and they are still on the floor, you know your feedback was not accepted. Feedback only works if it is accepted.

The "A" stands for actionable. If you told the teenager not to get the socks dirty in the first place it would not be an action item he could perform. Gelb says if the person cannot change or do something about the feedback it can be destructive.

The "R" stands for respect. Feedback must be given with respect. If the recipient feels the feedback is not genuine, then chances are such feedback will be ignored.

The "T" stands for timely. Telling someone the barn door is open after the horses have run away is not very valuable. In order for feedback to work it must be within the timeframe that someone can take an effective action.

In the iterative and agile process it crucial to keep circling back and get rapid feedback as you build functionality. It is essential that you know how to give and receive feedback. It can make or break a project.

Point 10: Risk First—Not!

Do the easy stuff first.

I received an email one day from a project manager and on the signature line at the bottom of the email it said to do the risky things first. This is balderdash. If you can avoid the risky things, don't do them at all.

"Do risky things first" is one of those catchphrases that project managers like to throw around, and maybe it is part of the project management conventional wisdom. The premise is that if you do the risky things first, the rest of the project will be clear sailing. On the other hand, you may think if you cannot get the risky stuff done, then the project will fail and you might as well know that upfront. In very rare cases, this might be plausible. For the majority of projects, though, the risky parts are not part of the baseline. Do the easy stuff first and get the benefits as fast as possible. Demonstrate results quickly. That is what the agile process is all about. Do it quick, do it smart, and do it simple.

Risk usually means something is both complex and expensive. Many times the most risky elements have no payback or are marginal at best. You need to assess requirements by cost, risk, and gain. A simple way to do so might be to take those index cards and sort them by gain and risk. Here you address the cards with the highest gain and the lowest risk first, and move through the pile from week to week. If another card comes in that has a better return on investment with a lower risk, substitute it. When you get to the end of the pile and all you have left is the high-risk, low-value items, throw them in the wastebasket and move on to the next project—one that has a better return with less risk.

One of the things that I always come back to is the 80/20 rule. Twenty percent of your functions will provide 80 percent of your benefit. It is higher in software, because that 20 percent is usually 10 percent of functions and the 80 percent is usually 99.9 percent of benefit. In the long run, if you do not do the risky stuff, most likely no one will even notice.

In Conclusion

Let's face it; everything is Internet-centric, both inside and outside the organization. As a result, the timing of IT projects around product life cycles has become much more critical. In the past when IT departments missed deadlines, no one liked it, but they often accepted it. But business has changed. Shortened application and information delivery times have become nonnegotiable. Accelerated product delivery from information technology is not only expected, but demanded. Everyone wants it yesterday. On the other hand, no one has any money and everyone wants to avoid risk. The agile process offers low cost, quick delivery, and low risk.

This lesson on the agile methods covered the following: Point 1 talked about the need for an iterative development style; it is the heart and soul of any agile process. Collaboration is part of all agile development processes, which was detailed in Point 2. Point 3 discussed rapid feedback, which promotes quickness and velocity. Velocity is a cornerstone of agile methods. Point 4 talked about how the agile process instills better testing and code quality controls than conventional software development. Point 5 considered using a Web-based standard infrastructure as a key component to the agile style.

No releases was the focus of Point 6. A no-release policy knocks down one of the software industry's biggest windmills. The next two points described the three most popular agile methodologies: Extreme Programming (XP), Rational Unified Process (RUP), and Scrum. Point 9 we discussed feedback and Point 10 rejected the notion of doing risky things first.

The agile methods are powerful tools because a few features are built, tested, and implemented at one time. This makes everything much simpler for the executives, users, and developers. Testers can test on an ongoing basis, quality is improved, and bugs and error are more controlled. The agile life is a wonderful life, but then geeks are easy!

Lesson Six: George Washington

Many stories are told about the first president of the United States, including Washington's statement: "Yes father, I did cut the cherry tree." Many have honored him for his truthfulness. However, George Washington never cut the cherry tree, nor did he say those words. It was also reported that he threw a dollar across the Potomac River. But actually, Washington was much too cheap to throw money around. Many claim that Washington was a great general. However, he lost more battles than he ever won.

Like all good project managers, Washington learned from his failures. He assessed his limited resources, found they were lacking, and formulated a strategy to overcome them. Of all the skills Washington possessed, perhaps his greatest was in project management proficiency. He knew the details of his army's skills, supplies, and position. He also knew the details of the opposing army's skills, tactics, strategies, supplies, and position. Washington was a master of logistics and he would become the model for modern generals to follow.

Washington was also a stickler for detail. For example, on his deathbed he told his doctor, "I am going. Have me decently buried and do not let my body be put into the vault in less than three days after I am dead." In grief, the doctor nodded. But this was not good enough for Washington. He asked him if he understood. The doctor replied that he did. "'Tis well," were his last words. Washington made sure that the listener grasped his communications. Good communicators make good project managers.

Many organizations have created an internal department, most commonly called the Project Management Office, or PMO, to formalize and professionalize project management expertise and leadership. One of the primary goals of these groups is to educate the organization on techniques and procedures necessary to run a successful project. This lesson covers project management expertise and the skills required to manage projects.

Point 1: Base Running

Just as every Little Leaguer knows you need to tag second before going to third, every project should follow project management fundamentals.

At Standish Group's first CHAOS University, the first speaker, Martin Cobb of the Treasury Board of Canada Secretariat, outlined this paradox: "We know why projects fail; we know how to prevent their failure—so why do they still fail?" In Cobb's talk, titled "Management of Large IT Projects in the Canadian Federal Government," he stated that the government had seen an increase in failure during the last year and a half. Of the 25 current projects, most were in trouble. So the Treasury Board set out to identify the issues and propose improvements to the management framework. It found five major issues: planning, execution, monitoring, procurement, and culture.

With the planning issue, the Treasury Board found that initial project definition was frequently inadequate; understanding, involvement, and support of senior management was often lacking; client focus was not sufficiently strong; and the Treasury Board submission and review process often did not work well.

Looking at the execution issue, the Treasury Board found that project management disciplines were not consistently applied, an experienced project manager was not always engaged, and changes were not managed rigorously.

With the monitoring issue, the board saw that regular sanity and health checks were not performed, progress was not always measured or reported, and accountability was weak or ill-defined. The traditional procurement approach was found to lack flexibility and was not conducive to cooperation. And finally, the culture issue discouraged open discussion and problem resolution. Failures were well advertised while successes were not. The board also found it had nowhere to turn since consulting in the public sector was not very strong.

Therefore, the Treasury Board set the following key principles in place: focused stages, problem definitions, preparation of the environment with stakeholders, and findings and execution. The Treasure Board also suggested the following approach: Manage in accordance with the benefits to be achieved. Emphasize the delivery of small projects within a defined vision. Utilize continuous improvement and rollout of solutions. Leverage the work and knowledge of others. Engage the community. And shoot—don't save—projects that are in trouble. The government took this framework and coupled it with some organizational changes to improve communications. Since that time the Canadian government has seen major improvement in its project results.

Point 2: Details

Keep track of the details.

Planning, enacting, and tracking a series of activities, tasks, changes, or functions to arrive at a goal are skills the project manager must maintain. As the centipede said to Alice in Alice in Wonderland, "If you do not know where you are going any path will take you there."

Features and functions must be considered individually as well as in relation to the whole. In other words, "the devil is in the details." Project managers who have an eye for detail, as well as an understanding of the big picture, will fare better than those who only have a grasp of the big picture. The big-picture-only view is for the executive sponsor; the project manager must have both a detail view and a big-picture view. For example, you must decide at the detail level what features and functions will be part of the project, and whether those features and functions will be for the first phase or for a later version. There must be a detailed change contingency plan in place with associated risk factors, cost increases or decreases, and gain increases or decreases.

You must be able to define the metrics, measurements, and stepping-stones (actual deliverables). Have an estimate of the resources per task and a plan to make the resources available. The dates of completion estimates of the stepping-stones should be based on the above information.

You must be able to organize project components into a working structure and then support that structure by having various functions contribute to the whole project. You must create and maintain a structure in which individuals cooperate systematically. Standish Group studies show that successful projects have project managers with good organizational skills and an eye for detail, while challenged and failed projects have project managers with fair to poor skills in these areas.

Point 3: Basic

It seems obvious that a project manager should have basic project management skills, but this is often not the case.

Many companies are assigning project managers to projects without the key skills needed to be a good project manager. Many of these key skills involve basic management proficiencies such as good judgment, diplomacy, and time management.

An investment in project management education, which is taught at many colleges and universities, may be needed. Private companies such as consulting firms offer formal classes, and the Project Management Institute (PMI) certifies professionals. The bottom line is that projects that have managers with good project management skills have a greater chance of success. Investing in classes and mentoring can go a long way. Many companies are now requiring their project managers to be PMI certified with a PMP or Project Manager Professional.

The project manager is the project's lynchpin. The IT community is just beginning to understand the true role of the project manager, the skills required to be a good project manager, and the benefits a project manager can bring to any project.

Project development environments are a microcosm of every organization, a mixture of people, processes, and products to produce a final outcome. Perhaps the most important trait project managers must have is the capacity to maintain a realistic vision for themselves, for the team, and for the entire company.

Many IT executives have confided in me that their best project managers came with business skills from outside the IT organization. There must be a core of experienced and competent project managers who can act as role models within the organization. More exposure to both the business organization and technical teams will increase the project manager's skills. Project management should be considered a profession, not a discrete task.

Standish Group's research clearly shows that projects are likely to be less challenged and more successful with a competent and skilled project manager on board. This, of course, can bring enormous benefits to an organization, such as reduced project expenses, higher company morale, and quicker time to market.

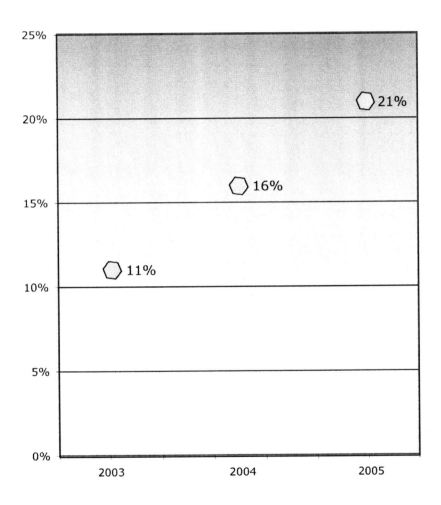

Chart 12

Do you require your project managers to have PMI certification or the equivalent?

Source: DARTS September 2003 to 2005

Point 4: Leadership

A project manager should be a good leader, another obvious point.

In John C. Maxwell's The 21 Irrefutable Laws of Leadership (Nelson Business, September 1998), he contends that leadership is a learned skill. The more you learn about leadership, the better leader you will become. His basic foundation is that leadership skill determines the fundamental level of a person's effectiveness. Maxwell argues that your leadership scope is how many people you influence, not how much organizational power you can wield from your position or office. Maxwell constructs his principles of leadership around 21 laws that include "Solid Ground," "Respect," "The Law of E.F. Hutton," "Intuition," "the Inner Circle," and many others. This is must read for any project manager.

It goes without saying that a project manager should be a good leader. You must have the basic leadership skills necessary to direct and pilot the stakeholders and technical teams. You need to lead project resources and bring those resources together. You must have the ability to lead at the detail level—establishing what features and functions will be part of the project—and whether those features/functions are for the first phase, for a later version, or not at all. There must be a change policy procedure in place, with associated evaluation of risk factors and cost increases. Change increases the scope of the project and the time involved, and it greatly increases the chance of failure. The project manager should advise the stakeholders about the risks of scope creep and its potentially disastrous effects.

Learning the word "no" is the hardest lesson for many project managers. Sometimes seemingly simple requests can put the project in real peril. All requests for changes should be characterized as baseline, yield, and non-yield. Each feature and function must be measured against business value, project quality, resources, risk, and the schedule. With 80 percent of delivered features and functions ultimately unused, enlarging the project's scope should not be taken lightly.

A project manager must be a hard driver, with the ability to focus on the goal and minimize diversions. He or she needs to lead by example in establishing the areas of accountability, responsibility, and authenticity. He or she must orchestrate all the resources so they play together like a fine symphony through leadership and project management skills.

Point 5: Connections

Project managers must be able to establish and maintain connections.

John C. Maxwell, who is also a protestant minister in addition to an author, claims the hardest group to lead is volunteers because they have no financial or security incentive to follow. There are exceptions, though. Max Schnur and his team began their project in January 2001; it was scheduled for completion in January 2002. Since it was all-volunteer labor, there was no cost. The project was completed in October 2001, three months ahead of schedule. What makes this story so incredible is that the leader was 15 years old. The challenges Schnur faced included communication, staff revolts, and task assignments around the globe, as well as coordination of graphics work with story lines and character development. In nine months, without money, permanent staff, and buildings, Schnur and his team created a major new game, The Darkest Day, to be enjoyed by users worldwide.

Connecting in the physical sense was not possible because developers were scattered across the globe. The team was truly international; participants were located in the United States, Pakistan, Australia, and throughout Europe. The game itself was international; it was played over the Internet throughout the world. So Schnur needed to connect in a different way. He did this by associating with the project's participants on a different level. He was their focus point and their caretaker. He connected to them by listening to them, asking them questions, solving issues, and giving them praise. He was an aggressive learner and energized the team through his example by providing needed technological and development advice. He was passionate about the project and let the participants feel his passion. He was clear and concise on the objectives and principles.

You must be able to clearly express and exchange thoughts and information to be effective in creating and maintaining connections. Research shows that successful projects have project managers with good communications skills, in contrast to challenged and failed projects. Good connections require good communications and good communications is one of the cornerstones of successful projects. You must communicate well, both verbally and in writing, to make connections. You might consider these two training venues to improve your connection skills: Dale Carnegie classes on how to win friends and influence people, and Toastmasters classes on presentation skills.

Point 6: Ownership

It's important to foster the sense of pride and accomplishment that comes with ownership of a project.

Promoting both an individual and a collective sense of ownership among team members will contribute to the success of a project. Commitment is stronger when team members become stakeholders who take personal pride in the outcome of the project. Consider the following five ways to help create a sense of project ownership: Clearly define roles and responsibilities; ensure the organizational model supports accountability; tie incentives to success; foster communication throughout the organization; and obtain commitment from project participants.

Each team member must understand his or her role on the team, and for which tasks they are responsible. Each task in the project plan should have an assigned owner. Create an organizational chart depicting both the chain of command and a high-level view of roles and responsibilities. Everyone on the team should understand the "big picture." Clearly defining roles and responsibilities will help prevent duplication of effort, as well as keep items from slipping through the cracks because of unclear ownership.

To assess preparedness in this area you need to consider several things. First, you must have an approved project plan. Second, you should be able to name all the decision makers. Third, you should have basic job descriptions for all your resources. You need to have the ability to assign resources based on descriptions of roles and responsibilities. Last, it would be great if you also have the commitment from all the team members to work with you on the project.

An effective organizational model must have defined roles and responsibilities that enforce accountability. Delegation of authority must precede enforcement of accountability. The staff will only be able to fulfill their assigned responsibilities if management delegates the appropriate level of authority. Each team should have a designated leader who is held accountable for the team. Each entity must have defined measures of success, which are communicated and understood by each person in the organization. One of the attributes that I like about Extreme Programming methodology is the built-in ownership of each participant and stakeholder.

Point 7: Team

The members of a project team are inclined to have a stronger commitment to the team if they feel their participation and contributions are valued.

The team members are the closest people to the project on an ongoing basis and should be encouraged to openly provide input and feedback. The team must also feel it has the support of the project leader, who must demonstrate commitment to the project and the team, in good times and — more importantly — in bad. The project must be viewed as achievable or broken into manageable subprojects or stepping-stones. It's important that you celebrate successes, even the little victories. A job well done may well be its own reward, but more tangible compensation in the form of money, promotions, or attendance at recognition events can substantially increase commitment from project participants. You want to make people feel they are part of your team.

When the New England Patriots played the St. Louis Rams in the 2002 Super Bowl, there was much controversy in New England over which of the team's quarterbacks would start. Now, I am not an expert when it comes to evaluating quarterbacks, but for those who rated Drew Bledsoe as a superstar and Tom Brady as less than so-so, why was the team losing that season with Bledsoe at the helm? When Bledsoe got hurt and Brady took over with the same players, the team won all of its remaining regular season games but one. The answer may lie in one simple but profound act: At the beginning of the Super Bowl, the St. Louis Rams announced their starting players by individuals, while the Patriots were identified as a team — by their request. Yes, as a team — all the players, coaches, and helpers.

This goes to the heart of project success and failure. All too often, organizations expect the superstar to pull the project off. All too often, the team is overlooked in favor of the player with the most talent. That certainly was the case for the New England Patriots. When Bledsoe was the starting quarterback everything revolved around him. After he was injured, the focus was spread to other players on the team. At CHAOS University, one participant said that TEAM stands for "Together Everyone Achieves More."

Point 8: Business Understanding

A grasp of basic business skills is one of the most important traits a project manager can possess.

"I had been an FBI agent throughout my career. Then my boss came to me and asked me to manage the Integrated Automated Fingerprint Identification System. I told him I was not up to the job. He replied that I was the model project manager," said Doug Domin of the Federal Bureau of Investigation. "I felt pretty good about this until my wife reminded me that a model was a miniature replica of the real thing." His wife's sarcasm aside, what made Doug the model project manager was that he understood the business from the inside out.

Standish Group research shows that project managers of successful projects have basic business operational knowledge and good business skills; while managers of challenged and failed projects possess less business expertise.

A good grasp of the business operations improves critical communication and translation among software designer, developer, users, and executive sponsors. A project manager needs to be able to envision project components and how the parts incorporate into the business as a whole.

The package of skills most executives we interviewed cite as desirable in a project manager include business knowledge, judgment, negotiation, good communication, and organization. Emphasis is on business knowledge. Moreover, project managers must not only know the business needs of their own company, but also those of their suppliers and partners.

Good communication is the cornerstone of successful projects, and if you know how to communicate in the language of the business your communication skills will improve. Project managers should be encouraged to use the organization's business dialect to keep communication simple and understandable to business-side management or sponsors. You should use simple terminology and avoid technology buzzwords and acronyms.

On the other hand, you also need to understand the technology to be able to talk to technical teams. You should have the skills necessary to converse with all the stakeholders and technical teams. The project manager needs to have a view of the project resources, how those resources come together, and how to help the business.

Point 9: Judgment

The ability to pass judgment on issues under consideration and reach a firm decision are vital project management skills.

Throughout the course of a project there are hundreds of decision points. Bad choices can lead to increased time and expense or outright failure. On the other hand, good choices can bring a project in on time and on budget. Projects need managers with good judgment and strong decision-making skills to succeed. Project managers, like other managers, often learn the hard way from their experience in the trenches and hopefully from past mistakes. Because of this, a project manager with previous failed and challenged projects could well be the best candidate for the next important project. On the other hand, this may just indicate poor judgment.

A project manager is much like a president of a small company, and like a president of a small company, he or she needs to have good judgment. The executive sponsor is the venture capitalist and he or she wants to invest in people with good judgment. The users are the customers and they want to buy from someone with good judgment. The developers are the workers and they want to work for someone with good judgment. Keeping the project on track is like keeping a small company on track. This is no easy feat and requires someone with good judgment.

In order to make the best judgments possible, you must control the resources and know all the project details. You must remember that each stakeholder is a professional and wants to be treated like a professional. You should establish the peer review process, set and focus on goals, and regularly communicate the project status in both meetings and reports to test your judgment.

You need to consider and judge things like proper incentives, cross-functional team analysis, and the team's defined responsibilities. You need to judge the team leaders' understanding and acceptance of their responsibilities. You need to consider the judgment of the steering committee and how it allocates resources. Project managers should be evaluated based on their project management skills, and good judgment is one of the essential skills.

Point 10: Seasoned

Green wood does not burn. A project manager's experience can factor heavily into the success of a project.

The best place to find a good project manager is from a project that has just failed," said John Gioia of program and project management consulting firm Robbins-Gioia. Failure is the best teacher. We learn more from our failures than we do from our successes. An experienced project manager will increase project success. It is true that a project manager is an additional expense, creates added paperwork for others, and is an intermediary between users and developers. Understandably, some have asked, "Why not just let the developers develop and let the users use?" Standish Group research clearly shows that application development projects will come in on time and on budget more often with an experienced project manager than those that have neither an unseasoned project manager nor a project manager at all.

A seasoned project manager sets the correct expectations early in the project with achievable stepping-stones. This can have a positive effect and demonstrate progress. He or she coordinates and motivates the stakeholders to create a successful project based on demonstrable results. He or she should be able to discourage over promising. A seasoned project manager should have learned that a happy stakeholder is one who is under promised and over delivered. An experienced project manager should be able to minimize project scope and create a better estimate. A seasoned project manager knows how to say no without creating controversy.

In The Standish Group's 1999 report, CHAOS: A Recipe for Success, we stated that the IT community was just beginning to understand the true role of the project manager, the skills required to be a good one, and the benefits he or she can bring to the project. Not only do CHAOS studies clearly show the benefits a project manager brings to a project, but since we began our research, project management has truly become a profession. For example, the Project Management Institute has a certification program that focuses on the skills required to be an effective project manager.

On the other hand, project managers are not superheroes. Projects are risky, and even a remarkable project manager cannot save a failing project. Project managers should be evaluated based on their project management experience and skills. The three most important skills that experienced managers have learned are communication, communication, and communication.

In Conclusion

Managing projects continues to be a daunting task amidst globalization that has brought about dispersed work forces and worldwide operations. Frequent business changes, new competitors, mergers, government mandates, and project staff departures can exacerbate an already delicate situation. To counter these issues you need to develop and maintain project management expertise.

Lesson Six covered project management expertise and the skills required to manage projects. In this lesson the 10 points began with the project management fundamentals. Point 2 considered keeping track of all the project management details. The third point covered basic project management skills. Point 4 looked at project leadership qualities and considered learning how to become a leader. Point 5 discussed getting and maintaining connections as an important part of managing the project to a successful conclusion.

Point 6 focused on the importance of fostering the sense of pride and accomplishment that comes with ownership. This includes promoting both an individual and a collective sense of ownership among the team, which contributes to the success of a project. Point 7 looked at how members of a project team are inclined to have a stronger commitment to the team if they feel their participation and contributions are valued. Point 8 talked about how a good grasp of the business operations improves critical communication and translation between software developers and stakeholders. Point 9 stressed good judgment, and why the ability to pass judgment on issues under consideration and reach a firm decision are vital project management skills. Point 10 considered the experience of the project manager in the success of a project.

Standish Group research clearly shows that projects that have the leadership and judgment of a talented project manager and an organization that supports its project managers, fare much better than those that do not have such capability and posture in place. However, we have to caution you about going too far. Take, for example, central governments like the United States and the United Kingdom. Both have dismal project track records yet high levels of project management competency. The New England Puritans believed in moderation in everything, and that goes to the heart of the project management process.

Lesson Seven: Diogenes the Cynic

Around 337 B.C., Alexander the Great went to visit Diogenes the Cynic in Corinth near Athens. There, he found the naked Diogenes sunning himself in a large tub. Alexander approached him and asked if there was anything he could do for the Greek philosopher. Diogenes replied, "Yes, stand aside. You're keeping the sun off me." Aides to Alexander were incensed and wanted to kill Diogenes for such disrespectful remarks. However, Alexander would not hear of it and remarked, "If I were not Alexander, I would be Diogenes." Whereas the outrageous philosopher quipped, "If I were not Diogenes, I would be Diogenes."

Diogenes believed that virtue was better revealed in action than in theory and made his life a protest against what he thought of as a corrupt society. In his pursuit of virtuous simplicity, he gave away his belongings and took up residence in that famous tub. He is said to have gone about Athens with a lantern in the daytime, claiming to be looking for an honest man—but never finding one.

When you begin a project, your CEO is the one holding the lantern. He or she is going to expect project managers to take their fiduciary responsibilities seriously. Good financial management can only come about through honest and frank estimates with correct risk and return assessments. The world has changed with the introduction of Sarbanes-Oxley and other accountability edicts. Management requires an honest financial picture.

The three pillars of project management are time, cost, and functionality. The key issue this lesson addresses is how business executives can forecast a return on their project investments realistically and honestly. There is no clear-cut, easy answer to this issue, but this lesson attempts to provide advice on some of the potential solutions.

Point 1: Accurate Estimates

Creating accurate estimates for a project is difficult, but critical.

In developing a more systematic approach toward project estimating, you need to face a bit of realism. Truly reliable estimates are rare birds. For more than a dozen years, Standish Group has accumulated almost 50,000 cases on the cost and resolution of projects. Using case-based reasoning technology, we have created a methodology to estimate project cost. However, it is no estimating panacea. Profiling one project against others to isolate costs is tricky and difficult at best, but this approach is much better than any of the alternatives, such as using outdated methods or thinking of ad hoc estimates that are seen to be attractive to sponsors or "safe" for management.

In focus groups, workshops, and surveys throughout the years, Standish Group asked IT executives what kind of payback they expected from new projects. The general consensus, derived from these research events, shows us that three-quarters of executives expect a return on investment within two years. However, this rate of return relies on one major element—an accurate estimate. Without an accurate estimate there can be no way to calculate a correct return. While we often mock that there are two types of estimates, lucky and lousy, in truth there are three: lowballing, sandbagging, and accurate.

Lowballing is used to get a project going. Sometimes this is intentional; other times it occurs because people are more optimistic and believe they can accomplish more for less in a shorter amount of time. Many consulting firms survive on the use of this technique to win bids, and then they get the client to change the specifications and requirements. Sandbagging is just the opposite of lowballing. Sandbagging is building in a big cushion so that you can come in low or on budget. Other times it occurs because people are more pessimistic and believe they need more time to complete tasks.

Accurate estimates require good tools, lots of historical data, experienced people, and good specifications. Standish Group uses five items to estimate a project: the client's estimate, a Standish general adviser estimate, a Standish Cost Advisor Specialist estimate, estimates from standard estimating tools, and profiles from our 50,000 projects.

Point 2: Marathon

Projects are marathons, not sprints, although in the case of the Scrum methodology they are made up of multiple 30-day sprints.

With most projects, you are generally in it for the long run. Suppose you are charged to chart the course for the Boston Marathon. Specifications state that it must begin in Hopkinton, Massachusetts, and end in Boston. Where would the course markers be set and at what intervals? If they are placed too close together, too much time will be spent laying out the markers. Placing them too far apart could cause a runner to go astray and lose time, potentially losing the race. You need to have the markers just right.

Milestones are too vague for application development projects. You need to work toward smaller stepping-stones and concrete deliverables. Each stepping-stone needs to have a cost, risk, and either savings or revenues over time limits associated with it. Maybe the new revenue forecasted over the collection of stepping-stones will only be good for two years and then will decrease to a minimal amount. You need to know if you can meet or beat these time limits. For example, if the project takes a year and a half to complete with any overages it could easily run out of the revenue time limit. Standish Group has seen many cases where this has occurred.

Project time frames are always aggressive. "I have never seen a project where they did not want it the day before we started," said Martin Edelman of Creative System Software. Expectations are subjective and sometimes have a propensity to mirror one's wants more than one's stated needs. A general rule of thumb is that one is usually willing to pay for what one needs. Pricing or costing each item and letting the stakeholders choose can provide a quick litmus test to differentiate wants from needs. One way to satisfy stakeholders is to deliver some functionality early. If you can deliver some high-value features and functions early on, then your payback begins earlier and increases your ROI. In terms of payback, the sooner the better, for time is the enemy of all projects, and money is the root of all evil.

Point 3: Lipstick

It's important to express the benefits of a project in the best possible financial light.

First, you must know your company's investment policy. For example, there is no universal standard for ROI or any agreed-upon mathematical formula. Many companies have their own standard policies. Many of these policies do include quasi-standard formulas, such as net present value (NPV), return on assets (ROA), return on equity (ROE), economic value add (EVA), and earnings per share (EPS). You should know and learn your company's ROI policy.

Once you know the ROI policy, the next item is a true cost estimate with time frames. You should keep in mind that many time frames are sensitive to market pressure, so if the project is delayed or late the ROI might not materialize. You should also remember that most estimates are inaccurate; I guess that is why they call them estimates. The next thing you need is the operating costs. This might be offset by not operating another system, but you need to know the differences between the two. Keep in mind you have training, consulting fees, lost productivity, new products, and many other expenses you need to include in your equation. The third big item is savings and/or increased revenue. You cannot have an ROI without one or both. Sometimes you need to dig hard to get all the savings and revenue items.

If the project does not meet the policy standard, then a decision needs to be made to change the project to meet the ROI objectives, either by removing marginal features or abandoning the project. You could also change the way you calculate the ROI; for example, you could capitalize items. I am not advocating "creative accounting"; all your projections should be in line with your organization's general accounting principles. The project needs to have real value and the value should be fairly measured in comparison to other projects under consideration.

Point 4: Budget

Create your project budget with stakeholder input.

In a CHAOS University workshop, we talked about how companies manage their information technology money. We first wanted to know how their IT budget process worked. The consensus was to start with a baseline and then add additional business needs and requirements. No one in the group used any other technique, such as zero-based budgeting. Zero-based budgeting is where the budget period starts with a clean slate and all items need to be justified. People who remember Jimmy Carter's presidency may recall how he tried to get the U.S. government to adopt this methodology. The only zeros we ever see from the "Feds" are at the end of the trillions of dollars spent or the number of successful projects.

The project budgeting process works best when users get involved. The CHAOS University participants felt if users were not part of the process, items were often missed and this caused problems during the project life cycle. Budgets where funding was fairly stable throughout the life of the project were much easier to control than budgets that fluctuated with the business, but they all agreed this was just a fact of life. They felt that they needed to have a budget replenishment policy of two to five years, to help smooth out spikes and dips. In all cases, the budget should be aligned with the business goals and investment strategies of the company.

Our CHAOS University delegates said cuts to projects are based on how badly the company needs the new functions, and the severity of the loss of service to the business of not having it. Most cuts are made to projects and new initiatives rather than cutting back work supporting current operational applications. However, users can influence where cuts happen, and here the squeaky wheel gets the grease. The best projects do not automatically survive a budget cut. So, if you have a project that can show a quick return on tangible savings, or better yet an increase in revenue, it has a good chance of getting or continuing funding.

If budget cuts do occur, you need to consider nonnegotiable items — differentiate the "must haves" from what items can be removed. Stakeholders need to be actively involved as decision makers in evaluating trade-offs. This enhances your chances of success.

Point 5: Break Even

Project managers need to find the break-even point.

Consider a project for an automated self-service order processing system, the justification for which was based on increased sales. Some of the savings might be lower phone costs, less person power required to take orders, fewer orders to enter, or even the elimination of a physical plant. Another savings might be the cost of printing, postage, and advertising, since much of the outbound marketing will be over the Internet. How will a reduction in these costs affect the ROI? Maybe the project includes setting up home workers and physical plant savings as part of the justification. Say, for example, a study has shown that these home workers are more productive. You calculate and add the increase in productivity to your savings.

You should know your break-even point. You also need to know what happens when you go beyond budget in order to be able to recalculate the payback period or breakeven point. Not knowing the answers to these questions could put you in peril if the project overruns time and money. There is an interesting math problem that you need to consider. Investment returns are like an airplane—it only travels forward and cannot go backward. What has been invested in the past is gone! Therefore, look at the breakeven point as today's estimated investment over the forecasted payback period.

The calculation for breakeven starts the minute the first dollar is spent on the project. You need to know the high- and low-value features and functions. If you can rank the features by value, you can start to affect the breakeven in a very positive way. You should tie all features and functions to the breakeven period. If you can put a dollar value on each feature and function, then you can begin to see a way for earlier payback. You should know what other projects are going on concurrently with yours and what the breakeven is for those projects. This is good information to know in case the company needs to scale back for one reason or another. If your project has a longer breakeven period than another project, it may end up on the chopping block. On the other hand, a project with a strong executive sponsor may survive over one that has a faster breakeven but a weaker sponsor. Also, a faster breakeven point rather than higher ROI percentage may be a better determinant of survivability.

Chart 13

In general, what kind of return on investment (ROI) do you expect from your in-house application development?

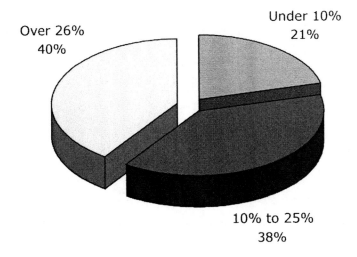

Over 26%
40%

Under 10%
21%

10% to 25%
38%

Source: DARTS 2005

Point 6: Change

Managing change is key to managing projects. The inability to do this well is almost always a major contributor to failure.

Change management is all about setting realistic expectations. The importance of this critical factor cannot be understated. Almost nothing can cause a misalignment between expectations and deliverables more quickly than a failure to manage change. The casual assessment of a verbal change request during a hallway conversation will almost certainly be neurologically processed by the user as a commitment to include the change at no cost, and with no impact to the original project schedule!

To determine whether you are effectively managing change and to prevent unrealistic expectations, you need to do the following: Make sure there is a clear statement of the requested change and the associated costs, risk, and gain. You should have a consultative and approval process in place to consider change requests. You most likely will need additional time and funding. You might have to move or delete some other requirements. That is why having a ranking by cost, risk, and gain is such a powerful tool.

It's important to have meaningful project stepping-stones, and they need to be set at frequent intervals to prevent irreparable errors if the project goes off track. In order to ensure meaningful project stepping-stones, you need to have the following items in place: Every stepping-stone has a demonstrable accomplishment or a measurable event, designed to ensure that the project is on track. You have a well-defined project life cycle or process methodology. That methodology needs to be consistently applied across the project and project portfolio. You need to define smaller "stones" for key tasks that could possibly impede achievement of the stepping-stones. You need peer and stakeholder reviews on a regular basis to ensure stepping-stones are being met. The review schedule should be adjusted to closely monitor trouble spots.

The stakeholders will usually place a higher value on items that satisfy their needs. Managing change can help avoid surprises and unmet expectations. You need to get the stakeholders to concur on changes in the prioritization and costs. You should have a process in place to continually capture and track stakeholder needs against cost and earned value.

~ My Life is Failure ~

Point 7: Incentive

Build in an incentive to finish the project on time and on budget.

Without an incentive to finish on time and on budget, projects end up like the Anglo-French Concorde Supersonic Aircraft project. That project was to design and build an airplane that would travel at supersonic speeds, thereby reducing travel time and cost. The plane would be a production model with a demand for more than 500 planes within 10 years of its first release. In addition, it was hoped that the new plane would jump-start Britain's fledgling aircraft manufacturing industry. The main project's executive sponsor was the British government, which set up a Supersonic Transport Aircraft Committee as part of the Ministry of Supply. The project manager was British Aircraft Corporation, with British Airways as the main user representative. Other major participants included the French government (sponsor), Air France, Rolls-Royce, and Sud-Aviation.

The design and prototype for the project started in 1963 and was expected to take three years, at a cost of $300 million (in 1963 U.S. dollars). The project actually took more than 10 years to complete and cost $2 billion. In 1968, the cost to build a production model was estimated at $10 million and rose to $23 million by 1973.

Originally there were going to be two models: a 150-passenger long haul and a 100-passenger short haul. The short-haul model was dropped. The cost to operate it turned out to be four times that of a similar-sized Boeing jet aircraft. Only 16 airplanes were built, at a cost of $250 million each (in 1978 U.S. dollars). If the planes were built at today's prices, each plane would cost more than $2 billion. None of these airplanes are still in service.

The Anglo-French Concorde project had everything going against it. First, it was a government-led project with two semi-cooperative governments. No market research was done that supported the demand for this type of airplane. There was poor communication between all the parties. The project initiators had no perception of the political impact from sonic boom noise, and the cost and time estimates were too optimistic. However, the biggest problem was the contractors were paid on a cost-plus basis with no incentive to finish the project on time and on budget.

Point 8: Bath

If a project no longer makes sense financially, pull the plug.

One of my accounting teachers once said to our class, when you have a customer who cannot pay you, the best thing you can do is go home and soak in the tub. The same advice applies to projects. If you reach the point that the project no longer makes sense, take the bath and pull the plug!

If that is the case, the people at the Bureau of National Affairs (BNA) must be good and clean. BNA's subscription and billing management systems did not reflect the current business. The system had been around for more than 50 years. In addition, changes were difficult to make and took a long time. It required more than 100 customer service representatives to support the legacy application. This old system did not let the salespeople enter orders, check status, or generate leads.

The solution was to build a new system that would allow their salespeople to do just that. The new system would also check renewals, allow for creative pricing, and respond to new products. It would, of course, allow for print, compact disc, and Web-based products.

The Phoenix project was the BNA's third attempt since 1972 to replace the current system. All prior attempts had ended in cancellation. The project started in the fall of 1995 and met the same fate as the previous attempts — it was canceled in the summer of 1997. There were few things done right in the project. There were many things done wrong. And even though management was engaged, it ignored the problem signs. The system was not tested, and modules were incomplete and did not work. BNA did not properly supervise the contractors.

BNA restarted the Phoenix project in the fall of 1997 under the code name Chrysalis. On this project the team used modern technology, purchased the infrastructure, and used small milestones as part of the development process. The project had a staff that knew the technology and could develop and support it. But that was not enough to make it successful. BNA had a tendency to continually increase scope and stray from its principles. Chrysalis was cancelled in 1999. BNA spent $5 million on Phoenix and another $1.5 million on Chrysalis. BNA continually recognized the project was failing and took a bath. At least the organization got that part right.

Point 9: Prune

If you're in charge of maintaining code, take a lesson from gardeners and prune it.

For the past few summers along the length of my garage at my Cape Cod home, I have had deep blue hydrangeas growing that are five feet tall and three feet deep. They are incredibly beautiful. I have had nothing to do with this event. I have a brown thumb. My wife of more than 35 years has a green one and she tells me that in the fall she cuts the stocks of the flowers down to about two feet. This allows new growth in the spring and the beautiful flowers by July. She also told me this is common practice in the gardening world. You trim trees, bushes, roses, and many other types of vegetation. You do all this to improve the quality of the plants.

This is rarely done to application software, but there actually is a fancy name for it. It is called code refactoring. Refactoring code basically cuts out unused code and trims the applications of meaningless functionality. The reason this is not done very often is twofold. First, the most significant reason is captured in this old saying in the software world, "If it ain't broke, don't fix it." The second reason encompasses priorities and money. It costs money to go back and take code out, so it is often easier just to move on and write new code. Both of these reasons ignore fundamental realities.

It is a fact of life that applications require maintenance and updating. The larger the code base, the harder it is to update, maintain, inspect, and test. By pruning dead code you allow new code to flourish. This, in the long run, makes code cheaper to maintain and test. In addition, bloated code uses more computer resources and decreases system performance. In refactoring, you are streamlining the code and thus performance will improve. It will be cheaper to operate and reduces your total cost of ownership. It is harder to find errors in bloated code and it will eventually break. Sticking with the philosophy of "If it ain't broke, don't fix it" only delays the inevitable. If your code is bloated it is already broken. You invest a lot of money in developing, testing, and deploying an application. Refactoring or pruning protects your investments.

Point 10: Pipeline

Instead of doing estimates for project costs, create a pipeline of projects, features, and functions.

If clairvoyance was a true science, then you could rely on traditional vehicles to estimate the cost of a project or group of projects. However, we all know this is both difficult and inaccurate. We get it wrong most of the time. Instead of doing poor and inaccurate estimates, why not create a resource pool? You most likely already have a resource pool—it is called your development staff. The cost of the pool is the budget for this staff. Now all you have to do is move output from the pool down the pipeline and into the hands of the stakeholders.

Changing from a project-based management structure to a pipeline-based management structure can be a nerve-racking experience, especially for the project mangers. In recent years project managers have been learning how to manage the process of projects. So it is not too far-fetched to believe you could learn how to manage a pipeline. The financial management of the pipeline is smooth, constant, and consistent.

Consider that you have a pool of 20 developers all using the Extreme Programming model. This would mean you have 10 developer pairs. Now pretend you have five stories or projects, and each project has 30 index cards, or 150 weeks of work. If you divide this work among your pool you will have 15 weeks of work.

If you mark each index card with its risks and gains, you can then sort them by their value. Of course, government mandates and political items may rise to top of the pool, but that is life in the big city. Each week you assess the progress, review your risk and gain assumptions, look at new requirements, and schedule the followings week's work. When the week's work is completed it is then moved to the testing area, checked by users and, if appropriate, put into production. This comes off really well in the no-release environment. In reality, the pipeline channels resources to the most valuable current activities.

In Conclusion

Taking a risk and gain approach to financially managing requirements puts everything in a different context. It creates healthier communication with the users and the stakeholders. Healthy communication is the cornerstone to project success. It is not whether a feature is wanted, but rather, what benefit that feature brings to the organization. Just like the old adage, "If you concentrate on the nickels, the dollars will follow," if you concentrate on the truly required features, the velocity of success and increased return on investment will follow.

This lesson on the financial aspect of software development projects first looked at the prospects of creating and maintaining accurate estimates and developing a more systematic approach toward project estimating and costing. Point 2 stressed that projects are marathons, and you need to prepare for the long run. Point 3 looked at ways to make your project more financially attractive. Point 4 talked about project budgets and how companies manage their information technology money. Point 5 discussed the financial break-even point and how that changes as a project moves forward.

Point 6 focused on managing change, and why the inability to do this well is almost always a major contributor to project failure. Point 7 suggested that offering incentives for finishing a project is a way to improve success and reduce failures. Point 8 discussed when to kill a project and take your lumps and losses. Point 9 considered the benefits of pruning or refactoring code to remove meaningless functionality. Point 10 looked at creating a functional pipeline of projects for consistent financial management.

I was doing a talk a few years ago in Sydney, Australia, for the Project Management Institute on project return on investment. One of the delegates raised his hand and said, "I am a project manager and I never did an ROI calculation, I just run the project. Why do I need to know all this stuff?" My answer then was, "The world is changing and financial management is becoming a big part of project management." It did!

Lesson Eight: New Model Army

Great Britain's King Charles I (1600–1649) and his archenemy Oliver Cromwell, a leader of the Parliamentarians, had been locked in a civil war for more than two years. The summer and fall battles of 1644 resulted in a stalemate. Cromwell, unhappy with the performance of the army in those battles, reinvented his army and gave the troops a new name: the New Model Army. The New Model Army went through months of special training, combat exercises, and battle simulations. Officers were schooled in battle strategies and tactics.

The Battle of Naseby took place on June 14, 1645, in Northamptonshire, England. Under Cromwell, the New Model Army, made up of 3,000 men, was deployed along a parallel ridge to battle Charles' Royalist troops, which numbered 10,000. The Royalists attacked along Cromwell's front line. Cromwell set a trap. Charles drove back Cromwell's left wing and followed them in pursuit as they fled. This allowed Cromwell's cavalry to attack and overwhelm the Royalists' position.

While the New Model Army lost only 200 men in what was its first encounter under Cromwell's newly formed army, the Royalists had nearly 1,000 dead and 4,500 taken prisoner. Perhaps this proves, once again, that a good plan executed by a well-trained and competent staff makes a big difference.

The mantra of executing a project plan is communicate, communicate, and communicate. However, you need to have ears tied to brains to hear the message. The best plan will fail if you do not have skilled and competent workers in sufficient quantity to complete the tasks at hand.

Point 1: Competency

Successful projects need smart, trained people.

The human resources component of "Management 101" emphasizes that the staff is your most valuable asset. Not surprisingly, one of the key project success factors identified in Standish Group's CHAOS research is a competent staff.

There are five key elements to ensure staff competency. First, identify the required competencies and alternative skills. Second, provide a good, continuous training program to enhance the staff skills. Third, recruit both internally and externally to provide a balance of experiences. Fourth, provide incentive to motivate the staff. Finally, ensure the staff is project-focused.

To ensure a competent staff, you must understand the project. You should know the range of activities to be undertaken in the project and be able to match skills with those activities. Certainly you will need a variety of resources, possibly a project executive, an administrator, technical resources, and testers. The challenge consists of properly identifying the required competencies, the required level of experience, and the expertise needed for each identifiable task. You will need to understand the number of resources needed with a given skill, and when these will be needed. This is a balancing act in itself. Additionally, consideration must be given to whether the skills are available in-house or can be developed, taught, or bought, and whether they will be available when needed. Soft skills, such as "works well with others" and "communicates effectively," are equally important when identifying required competencies and must not be ignored, as they are also essential to project harmony.

Mentoring offers a human strategy to increase competency and builds confidence in newly learned skills. A mentor can serve as part of a positive approach to workforce development and, at the same time, establish a preventative posture against risk. Mentoring should be part of every organization's training and skills development program, and mentoring time should be built into project planning. Create support systems and tools that help novices convert shaky new skills into competent mastery. Provide opportunities for workers to compare ideas and lessons learned about mentoring with other staff members. Finally, look at every new project as an opportunity to increase team competency.

Point 2: Position

Projects are a team sport. In a team environment, everyone should know his or her place and position.

In baseball, the pitchers pitch and the catchers catch. You need to assign team members to a specific task or set of tasks according to their strengths and talents. Each individual's role is essential to the overall process and they should understand the importance of their positions.

There is a sequence to success. By nature, project management is a perilous journey with potential potholes and roadblocks lurking around every corner. With shortened time frames from order to delivery, the most difficult aspect of administering a project is not the destination, but the journey. Without each team member knowing his or her position and having the proper planning, preparation, or practice, a project can collide with failure at any point.

Planning includes identifying and obtaining the right positions for the project, ensuring availability of sufficient resources, and providing training, if necessary. The plan should identify the positions needed for each stepping-stone. If the resources are not available, then the project or plan needs to be changed to reflect reality. Timely resolution of position conflicts must be address and resolved.

Unfortunately for project managers, time is a backseat driver — a constant reminder that deadlines loom over the horizon. Unlike an auto race, a project's end result is often uncertain. The execution of a successful project requires position strategy. This strategy needs to be plotted against project roadmap and position coordinates. You need to know who is in your project pit crew. If a position goes away, the repercussions can cause irreparable damage to the overall effort. The emphasis is on teamwork. Projects require group effort as much as individual contribution. In a race, seconds count. A pit crew chief depends on the ability and responsiveness of his team to be able to resolve problems instantaneously. One loose lug nut can lose the race. The same scenario applies to projects. Whoever assumes the driver's seat must ensure consistency and coordination throughout the entire project team and manage the talent he or she has on the team.

Point 3: Motivation

The use of individual and team incentives has become a popular tool in motivating achievement of project goals or significant stepping-stones.

To be effective, the incentives must be meaningful and must be earned. If the project leader always gets an award, or if team awards don't take into account individual levels of contribution, the incentive program loses credibility. Everyone on the team should have an equal opportunity for recognition. It's important to understand what motivates your staff: Is it money? Attendance at a special seminar or conference? The opportunity to work on a certain project? Promotions? Incentive programs should be communicated with clearly defined attainment criteria tied to the project's success.

Consider the following questions when assessing or implementing an incentive program for a project: Are there rewards for the achievement of company, team, and individual goals? Are staff "hot buttons" identified? Are the rewards given judiciously? Are the measurements that are chosen tied to the project's success? Are the incentives communicated to everyone?

One of the most effective ways to manage expectations is to ensure that the project plan clearly identifies and defines all deliverables. Each phase of the project should have a set of deliverables and require a sign-off before proceeding to the next phase. A requirements document should not be delivered at the end of the project, but rather at the beginning when its value is greatest. A deliverable should be small enough to be attainable, such as a code function versus an entire module. Project deliverables are often documents or plans, and the format and contents of this type of deliverable should be discussed and agreed upon. Standard conventions should be established and communicated to the team. Status meetings should always include a review of what has been completed and what deliverables are due.

The size, nature, and intervals of incentives may vary. For instance, a project manager may choose to use both individual and team incentives, or strictly team incentives. At any rate, the use of incentives must be a means to an end, but the pursuit of the incentive should not become an end in itself. The key to incentives is to have well-defined goals and a mechanism for self-evaluation so that everyone can gauge his or her performance against the goals.

Point 4: Togetherness

There is a vast difference between having a group of individuals work on a project and having teamwork on a project.

Volumes have been written about the power of teams. Team-building workshops flourish. Teaming implies a codependent relationship — "all for one and one for all." Championship athletic teams are perhaps the best illustration of high-performing teams. Each person has a defined role, but all members have a common goal. Individual success is tied to collective success. A single player can become the MVP, but it takes the whole team to win the championship. "Team Building 101" stresses having the team establish ground rules governing how it will operate. Communication is the key to success with any team, and team building requires the active participation of every member. Some teams utilize a "contract" to gain individual commitment to the team.

Project teams often face unexpected changes and developments that require them to make prompt, effective decisions. You should encourage creative thinking and help your team fully consider all alternatives to reach the best solution. Before your team can make effective decisions, you must first clarify what you want to accomplish. Make sure to put those goals in writing and keep them in front of everyone throughout deliberations. For project-critical decisions, it's vital to consider all possibilities. Encourage your team to think creatively, no matter how outlandish some ideas might seem. Carefully weigh all the pros and cons, and consider each alternative's potential impact on everyone involved in the project. Finally, be certain your team has the facts it needs to make well-informed decisions.

You should consider the following basic items as food for thought to help strengthen a project team: Create an environment of openness, honesty, and trust. All members of the staff should be treated fairly. On the other hand, each member should know his or her job. A mentoring process can have real advantages so that senior members can help develop junior members. Management should encourage and foster respect among the team and across teams. It is also healthy to periodically evaluate how well team members are working together. In the XP process, for example, pairs move around to help create and spread expertise and to generate a sense of a greater team.

Point 5: Training

Ongoing staff training can benefit current projects and contribute to the pool of skills available for future projects.

Staff development is a major issue for many IT executives and application development managers. Of particular concern is the training and competency in the never-ending flood of new technology and current technology upgrades.

Training for team members should be factored into the project plan, and the training should meet several objectives. First, the training must be relevant. For example, a team working under time constraints will be frustrated by getting pulled off the project to go to a class that the members deem to be of no value. Second, management's commitment to ongoing training must be genuine. It's easy to allow the project to take precedence over everything else—education, vacation, and so on. This can hurt a project in the end, particularly a long-term project. Third, the quality of the training instructors is important. Instructors need to be able to relate the subject matter to "real world" experiences and help the staff identify ways to apply the knowledge to real projects. Fourth, the skills taught need to be utilized on current projects. Fifth, you need to hold staff members accountable for developing their skills. And finally, have a process in place to develop soft skills such as communications.

Lawyers, like many professionals, shun the thought of training, and for an IT department, organizing training is like herding cats. O'Hagan, Smith and Amundsen (OSA) is a midsize law practice that relied upon new technologies. The firm needed to set up a formal program to educate the staff, but the staff resisted, claiming they did not have the time. The managing partner was the key to getting the participation. He was the first to participate in the formal program and pass the tests. He insisted that all staff members go through the same program. By the completion of the program, most lawyers were doing the majority of their tasks through the new system. Because OSA was able to reduce its support staff by 10 people, the resulting ROI was 470 percent. This is a perfect example of where education can pay back big dollars.

Point 6: Mentoring

Good mentoring can improve project success rates.

In ancient mythology, Odysseus entrusted Mentor with the education of his son, Telemachus. The concept of mentoring has since been used to define a constructive relationship between individuals, with the purpose of providing support, guidance, and assistance to individuals in the achievement of their full potential. The role of the mentor encompasses friendly advisers, coaches, and teachers who are entrusted with the education and development of entire organizations. They possess advanced, or expert, knowledge in a particular field, and can expose organizations to new ideas and important trends in industry best practices. Like their predecessors, today's mentors share skills, knowledge, and experience. They are expected to model desired behaviors and processes that enable the organization to achieve higher performance levels.

There are 10 fundamental questions you can ask when evaluating a professional mentor. First, what direct experience does the mentor/contractor have? Has the mentor addressed similar challenges, achieved similar objectives, or solved complex, system-wide problems? Second, given the understanding of the current situation, has the mentor/contractor proposed constructive suggestions and/or strategies? Third, what methodologies has the mentor/contractor offered? Have they been used successfully in the past? Are references provided? Fourth, what training has the mentor/contractor received to perform the role of mentor? Are they technically qualified? What was the duration of training or the credentials earned?

Fifth, what are the characteristics of the mentor/contractor? What are their personal or team attributes (i.e., aggressive, driving, challenging, or passive, patient, empathetic)? Sixth, what are the greatest strengths of the mentor/contractor, and why? How are these relevant to the company's needs? Seventh, in which areas is the mentor/contractor weak, and why? Eighth, during the selection process, has the mentor/contractor made observations or suggestions for immediate change? Are these observations viable? Ninth, why does the mentor/contractor want to work on this assignment? If there are incompatibilities, can a change be requested? Tenth, has the mentor/contractor answered any questions that should have been asked, but weren't? What additional information has the mentor/contractor offered?

Selecting the best professional mentor is critical to the ongoing success of any program and improving project success rates.

Point 7: Chemistry

Chemistry is hard to define, never mind manage. It is one of those things that you know when you have it, and it's painfully obvious when you do not have it.

We have all seen enough TV programs and movies to recognize good and bad chemistry. Some actors just work better together. The same is true with project team members. Building and maintaining team chemistry is an ongoing process, which should include participation from the team. Each member needs to clearly know his or her roles and responsibilities. The staff needs to be properly motivated and have the proper skill set.

Human nature appears to be such that we take much better care of things we own. The rental car industry has amassed countless stories of how customers don't take care of rental cars, particularly if the car is a business rather than personal expense. Promoting a sense of staff ownership can only benefit a project and help to create positive chemistry. It strengthens the bond between people when they have a common, vested interest in the success of the project. The automobile manufacturer Saturn is a prime example. Saturn has successfully promoted a bond between its employees and customers, and most of Saturn's advertising shows individual employees demonstrating their sense of pride in each vehicle they manufacture, as well as pride in the team that built it.

A major problem IT departments must contend with during a corporate consolidation is how to maintain the staff chemistry. Mergers and acquisitions, of course, create undue pressure on IT organizations with respect to managing their operations and expectations. But now they must deal with the monumental task of melding two different corporate cultures and creating new chemistry. There is no proven method, just trial and error. You may have a better chance with people with the same level of expertise, but this is not a surefire solution.

The Extreme Programming pair system can help identify who works better together. Constant and consistent communication with the staff is absolutely vital to maintaining good chemistry. Simply allowing people to voice an opinion about who they like working with can make a significant difference. You continuously need to monitor and make sure the chemistry of the team is right.

Point 8: Toxic

As the saying goes, there is one in every crowd.

You will often encounter team members who are exceptionally difficult to deal with, and you are frequently forced to work with them under stressful conditions. Knowing how to manage a toxic developer or stakeholder could be very influential to the success of a project.

Sometimes you just want to strangle someone. But of course, that's not an option. What you need to do is talk things out. You should not let problems worsen because it is unpleasant to talk about your concerns candidly. Pull your difficult team member aside for a conversation. You do not have to be confrontational to be effective. Squarely address the specific actions that are having a damaging effect on the team, and ask for ideas on how to make things better for everyone.

Spend some time in an informal setting, maybe over lunch, talking with your team about personal interests and goals. Every team usually has one member who gets along with the toxic person. Watch how he or she deals with your problem team member, and pattern your own behavior after his or hers. Encourage other team members to do the same.

If one person seems bent on creating trouble, try to find a new, more constructive target for his or her energy: finding a way to meet an impossible deadline, for example, or solving an especially difficult problem. Or, assign that person to a sub-team of people he or she works best with, and give that group a task that makes the best use of each member's skills and talents.

On the other hand, it might just be you! Maybe you do not like this person. You might consider the benefits of self-reflection. You might have to change your own behavior and attitude to deal with this person. If you have an unusually high number of problem teammates, some somber soul searching is necessary. As you conduct your skills inventory, you also might notice what you are doing right. Watch for actions and words that generate positive reaction from the problem child, and make a point of continuing them in your ongoing relationship. On the other hand, if the chemistry is too toxic, maybe that person should be someplace else.

Point 9: Turnover

Turnover disrupts projects; keeping a team intact requires speed and good management.

"You are going to lose good people," said Bob Kelley, former CIO of Biopure. Turnover can wreak havoc with a project. Loss of critical talent can delay the project for weeks or even months. It can cause mistakes and errors that will have a negative impact on the user acceptance. It can cause the project to fail. It is important to retain the team throughout the life of a project, if possible.

There are obviously no quick fixes or easy answers to retaining a quality staff. Things that help are a good working environment, interesting things to work on, friendly staff, stock options, free coffee, and a competitive wage. Geeks like to dress down, but almost everyone allows that in their shops these days. Training and seminars may help to motivate someone to stay with your organization. In addition, goal-specific incentives and bonuses may help to keep staff members around until the end of a project.

There are three techniques that have proven ineffective in maintaining a team throughout the life of the project. The first poor technique is vague or false promises. This tactic may work for politicians, but never for IT professionals. They are too demanding and precise. The second dreadful technique is offering pep talks. Enduring a project meeting is torture enough without having to deal with management saying, "Remember gang, there's no 'I' in 'team'!" The third ghastly technique is poor planning. No clear course of action leads to uncertainty. Uncertainty can ultimately lead to mutiny.

Project managers have always understood that their greatest challenge is to create and maintain a harmonious team of people who are also in harmony with the products and the process involved with the project. Embracing an agile methodology with a standard infrastructure can greatly reduce the challenges of maintaining a team. In the confines of today's rapid development environments, instilling this understanding throughout the entire organization should be one of your highest priorities. Therefore, the project management community should embrace one of the simplest and most powerful tools: speed. The faster the project gets resolved, the less likely the team will turn over. Time is the enemy of all projects, and speed is your defense.

Chart 14

In your opinion, what is the percent of turnover of key stakeholders within a project completion cycle?

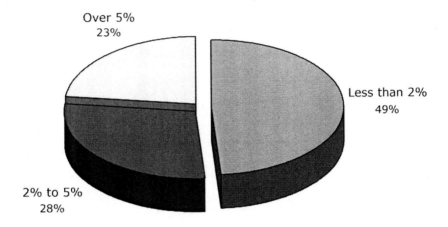

Over 5%
23%

Less than 2%
49%

2% to 5%
28%

Source: DARTS 2005

Point 10: Schucker

Consider Schucker's secrets to success in dealing with staff and staff issues.

In a December 2001 CHAOS University session, Foster Schucker, CTO of Kaloke Technologies, presented his theory for successful operations. Since Kaloke Technologies is a small company, Foster spent some time talking about effectively managing people, time, and money. There are five major points to Schucker's secrets to success.

The first, Schucker said, is that people are number one. Hire people with very basic skills and, most importantly, who can learn fast. Also, make sure that the people on project teams have — and are willing to participate in — social interaction. Working with small, focused teams with anywhere from three to 11 people is best.

Second, team members have to be enthusiastic about what they are working on. Be sure to hire people with a good work ethic, especially telecommuters who need to get up in the morning and get moving. If people are not motivated, this will really snag a project. Schucker also emphasized the fact that self-improvement is necessary in all employees. Team members should be constantly saying, "Look what I can do!"

Third, treat everyone alike — from contracted employees to top executives. Contractor offices and workstations look just like those of other employees at Schucker's company, even his. Also, give everyone the same flexibility in work times, locations, and tools used.

Fourth, conduct a lot of peer reviews, where coworkers take a look at each other's code and evaluate it. Peer review can often minimize the amount of testing necessary, and can sometimes be more effective than testing.

Last, manage time and don't let people waste it. Be sure to get needed information now, because there may not be a later. Schucker also said that building prototypes is essential, especially for customer interfaces and for those tricky bits of code that others are not sure about. Time savers include automating repetitive tasks, and building a tool for those actions that have been learned so that they don't have to be relearned. Other time savers include planning for testing, making sure to test early and often.

~ My Life is Failure ~

126

In Conclusion

There are no projects without people. Projects are made up of people. There are no issues except people issues. The quality of outcome depends directly on the quality of the staff involved in the project.

Lesson Eight on skilled resources addressed the major application development staff issues and the issues around their support systems. Point 1 looked at the notion of competency and what you need to consider in evaluating the competency of your staff and the team. The second point was all about position and the placement of workers in the jobs that will benefit the project. The third point discussed using incentives as a tool for motivation to achieve project goals or significant stepping-stones. Point 4 covered team building and keeping the team together. The fifth point centered on staff development and training programs.

Point 6 advocated the use of mentors and mentoring to improve the skills and competency of staff members and the team. Point 7 looked at how chemistry between team members can affect the project, in both positive and negative ways. Point 8 was on dealing with an exceptionally difficult team member. Point 9 discussed the effect of turnover on the project and ways to minimize it. The lesson closed with some advice from Foster Schucker, CTO of Kaloke Technologies, and his theory for successful projects through skilled staff.

When a project has both teamwork and skilled resources, it can prevail under even the most dire circumstances. The Mizuho Bank's EFT project participants, for example, were stationed on the 50th floor of the World Trade Center in Tower One on September 11, 2001. Fortunately, for one reason or another, not a single member of the team was at the World Trade Center that day. Like many people in America and around the word, this tragedy had a major impact on the Mizuho Bank's people and their priorities. In addition, with the collapse of the building, physical equipment and some of the software changes were destroyed. The team was forced to move into the disaster recovery data center in Jersey City. This site was not favorable for project development. The offices were small and cramped, and the other workers there were trying to keep up with daily bank work. The EFT team had limited access to computers. Even with all these obstacles, the team pulled together and completed the project only 45 days behind schedule. This story is testament to the importance of skilled resources and teamwork.

Lesson Nine: War Room

Winston Churchill said, "This is the room from which I will direct the war." The prime minister was referring to the secure room in a basement chamber located near Whitehall and 10 Downing Street. The bunker was created because of the relentless enemy bombings. During the height of World War II it operated 24 hours a day, seven days a week. It became the center of all major military activity in the United Kingdom. In this room, Churchill met with advisers, cabinet members, and military intelligence officers and made some of the most serious decisions of World War II.

Churchill and the "war room" are forever linked in our minds as much as his long cigar and round hat. The concentration of executives, information, and experience helped Britain, in the darkest hours of the war, prevent a German victory. We, too, are in a war and we are losing it. Standish Group's latest CHAOS numbers show only 28 percent of IT projects come in on time and within budget. The bombs fall every day. However, they come in all different forms. From users, they look like additional requirements; from the executives, they look like changing business goals; and from the developers, they look like the latest technical fashions. We need a war room. The war room of IT is called the Project Management Office.

The PMO or war room is the keeper of the methodologies. Methodologies are a set of policies, procedures, standards, processes, practices, tools, techniques, and tasks. They can be bookshelves of theory or, my favorite, a one-page description of the process. In most cases they are just common sense ways of doing projects that can lead to success. While a PMO represents the most formal of methodologies, you can implement methodologies without a PMO.

~ My Life is Failure ~

Point 1: Black Tie

Often black tie is more appropriate than business casual.

Over the past number of CHAOS University events, no subject has had more time devoted to it than formal versus informal project methodology. First, it is a difficult task to define where informal leaves off and formal begins. Second, how much is too much? Can there ever be enough, or does the formal process cause paralysis through analysis? Third, what are the trade-offs? What are the costs to document? Is this time away from real work? A CHAOS University participant from America Online claimed that the formal process stifled creativity, and that creativity was a major factor in the company's success. However, it is clear from Standish Group research that the right amount of formal project methodology can improve success. Except for the government sector, those firms that use a formal methodology have almost twice the success rate than those firms that do not have formal methodology.

There are basically three minimal things every project should have: a problem statement, a requirements document, and a project plan. I recommend the following actions in developing these items. First, create a problem statement with the essential user involvement. Second, produce a requirements document with definitions and functional specifications. The requirements document should be defined in a language the user understands, with a clear focus on the business problem the project intends to solve. Third, craft a project plan. The project plan should include a concept of the solutions, the names of the personnel involved, and the assigned roles and attainable stepping-stones.

The main objective is to get where you want to go according to the details in the project plan. Project management is essentially a business within a business. You are managing a small business within the company. A project executive faces the very same issues the company grapples with, such as budgeting, personnel, scheduling, and operational overhead. Because today's projects are more complex and require rapid results, companies that do not implement measures to maintain project continuity have a greater chance of failure.

Chart 15

How often do you setup a checkpoint system
to ensure project consistencies?

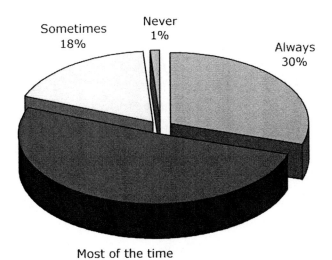

Sometimes
18%

Never
1%

Always
30%

Most of the time
51%

Source: DARTS 2005

Point 2: Problem Statement

Every project plan must have a problem statement, ensuring that everyone is trying to solve the same problem.

A complete problem statement with which the stakeholder community can identify will have the following attributes: The problem statement should be written in business terms and be tied to a business process. The problem statement should have a definition of the business problem. The problem statement should address root causes and not just symptoms of the problem. The overriding key to the problem statement is that everyone has to be solving the same business problem.

Lack of a clear problem statement that all agree on can derail a project. For example, in 1992, IBM was losing the UNIX transaction business to Tuxedo, now owned by BEA. IBM needed a product to compete. Around that time, I was sitting at a horseshoe conference table at IBM Laboratories in Hursley, England. Phyllis Byrnes, head of the lab, was giving a presentation on a new product, to be named CICS/6000. At the time, IBM's CICS S/390 product generated close to a billion dollars per year for IBM. It is one of the most successful software products of all time. So, in the early 90s, IBM began a project to create a UNIX version of CICS.

Then Byrnes showed a slide illustrating that CICS/6000 was being built over IBM's Systems Network Architecture (SNA). I then pointed out to Byrnes that the new CICS/6000 was being developed over the Distributed Computing Environment (DCE), not SNA. Ellen Hancock, president of IBM's Network Computing Division at the time, was sitting three seats to my right. She beamed up and told me I was wrong. The two people between us hurried out of the way. I then turned, looked her straight in the eyes, and told her in no uncertain terms I was right and she was wrong. People did not normally tell Hancock that she was wrong! She had specifically made a strategic decision to implement the new product over SNA. But it was too late; Hancock did not learn of the developers' decision to use DCE until the product was close to being launched into the marketplace.

The problem was, the project didn't have a common problem statement. Marketing was trying to sell more CICS, but the developers were trying to create the world's best-distributed computing environment. Both sides lost. CICS/6000 was one of IBM's poorest-performing products and DCE was a mammoth failure.

Point 3: Requirements

All project methodologies should include a formal process of gathering and maintaining requirements.

Requirements management is the process of identifying, documenting, communicating, tracking, and managing project requirements, as well as changes to those requirements. It is not a single point in time occurrence, but rather must be an ongoing process that stays in lockstep with the development process, especially iterative agile development. Losing sight of requirements is often the first step on the road to over-budget, late projects that do not meet specifications, or end up canceled.

In 1994 the Software Engineering Institute (SEI) released version 1.1 of its Capability Maturity Model® (CMM), a process framework intended to help achieve software development process improvements. The CMM identifies five levels of maturity for an organization and provides guidance on key processes related to each level, to assist organizations in progressing from the base level to the top level. One of the key process areas associated with level 2, also known as the repeatable level, is requirements management. The SEI defines the objective of requirements management as ensuring that customer requirements are the focus of the project, from inception to delivery; they must be communicated, documented, and analyzed. Any changes must be tracked with corresponding updates made to project documentation and plans. The CMM advocates a hand-in-glove relationship between the requirements and the project and, along with ISO 9000, has become an industry standard.

Common sense dictates that the earlier an error is detected in the development cycle, the less costly it is to fix. In business-critical environments, the cost of an application error can be staggering. In fact, most IT executives will acknowledge that poor requirements cause more than 10 percent of quality issues. The potential price tag can include lost business, lost opportunity, and deteriorating image, leading to a quantifiable dollar impact that could surpass the imaginable. There are high costs not only to finding and fixing errors in a deployed production system, but in distributing the revised software to hundreds or thousands of remote users. These costs are particularly painful when root cause analysis results determine that errors could have been avoided altogether, or identified sooner through a formal requirements process.

Point 4: The Plan

A detailed project plan helps to prioritize critical project activities, minimize disruption to normal business, and enhance collaboration among all project contributors.

Once it is determined that there is a clear business problem and you know your requirements, you need a plan. The project plan should include a description of the project scope, a list of activities, a schedule, time estimates, cost estimates, risk factors, resources, assignments, and responsibilities. To ensure that your project plan is viable and easily understood by all involved, ask the following questions: Has the plan obtained buy-in, and have all stakeholders signed off? Have estimates been made based on experience? Is the plan based on a mature process (life cycle, template)? Does the plan include realistic stepping-stones and time frames? Is there a mechanism in place to continually review and modify the plan as part of the process? Is there a kill switch in place?

Apple Computer had worked for years on a new operating system code-named Copeland. The problems were many; for example, there were no plan reviews, and no statistics on code, testing, and functions. Completion dates were determined by marketing, without development input. The entire project was done top-down rather than with engineer buy-in. Even if the new operating system were completed, it would not meet customers' needs and had less functionality than the current system, which was stable. Soon after IBM's Ellen Hancock went to Apple as the company's chief technology officer, she terminated the Copeland operating system project. However, the same team was able to successfully revitalize the current system until a new operating system was launched, which is the magnificent OS X. The key was that Hancock put together a plan and she worked the plan.

Project managers need to conduct frequent and open reviews to inform all the stakeholders of the project status. Maintaining a solid communications network helps identify target stepping-stones, delegate assignments, and address concerns. You need direct access to the decision makers, whether they are executives or users. This level of interaction helps to process or channel important administrative decisions. When executing a plan, if you encounter a variant, you must have controls in place to accommodate necessary changes or alterations to the project strategy.

Point 5: Butterfly Effect

Remember the butterflies.

At the March 2002 CHAOS University, Carlos Colino, formerly of e-Global, presented his project case on the development of the "Payment Factory" (Factory). The Factory is a service bureau created by a consortium of Mexican banks and other financial institutions, such as Banamex and Bancomer, to process merchant credit card payments. The idea of the Factory started in February 1998. By March 2002, the Factory was processing more than 1.3 million electronic transactions per day. At the time of this presentation the new service bureau commanded a 62 percent market share in Mexico. This did not come about easily.

Colino summed up the major lessons learned through overcoming the project's challenges as the "Butterfly Effect." As applied to weather conditions, it is said when the butterflies fly in Tokyo, three days later there will be a major storm in San Francisco. In other words, small details and mistakes can signal major problems. If such details are ignored, they can accumulate and result in major catastrophes. Another part of the "Butterfly Effect" is to have a thorough understanding and knowledge of the current state of the business. While experience is helpful, it is not always an indicator of current knowledge. A holistic understanding of the current state of the business climate, including competition, is much more important than experience.

The third part of the "Butterfly Effect" is keeping track of all the butterflies. In any given project there could be hundreds, even thousands, of butterflies. These butterflies could be suppliers, contractors, users, customers, executives, or team members. Any one of these butterflies can create a small problem that could turn the project into chaos. Colino recommends staying close to all your butterflies.

The fourth part of the "Butterfly Effect" is passion. Colino recommends you have a strong passion for your work and the project. Make sure the job is fun and exciting. Believe that everyone is equal, important, and part of the decision-making process. Engender a high degree of mutual trust and support among the team members. Set up standards and goals and work together to reach them, while rewarding achievements. Use the formal methodology to talk freely and openly, handling conflicts as they arise.

Point 6: Making Tea

Consider the use of analogies to improve communication between users and developers.

The eScience Semantic Grid's goal is to give the scientific community greater access to experiments and data created by individual scientists. The scientists or chemists we are writing about use very modern and state-of-the-art tools to carry out their experiments. These scientists create volumes of data on hypotheses, methods, testing, amounts of chemicals used, and the methods for combining them. They spend countless hours analyzing the success or failure of their results. Yet, the way most of these chemists recorded their experiments go back to almost cave drawings.

These chemists recorded their experiments in a paper notebook called a lab book. The only people who had access to their research until it was published in research papers were other chemists who were close at hand. The idea was to automate the lab book to allow for greater access and data mining. On the information technology side came professionals from various fields of computer science. The computer science team included talented individuals in Web information systems, grid computing, intelligent agents, Web services, and human computer interaction.

This may sound like an easy project, but it was not. The problem was the users (the chemists) and the developers (the computer scientists) did not speak the same language, even though in this set of circumstances it was the Queen's English. The developers would ask a question and the chemists would answer it, but it was plain from both sides that the chemists did not understand the question or developers did not understand the answer.

In order to bridge the gap, a group from the University of Southampton created the Smart Tea Project. First, the developers would make tea and explain what they were doing at each stage of the tea making process. Then the chemist would make tea and explain the process to the developers. From this simple analogy they developed a common understanding and were able to move the project along with great success. For more information about this project, go to smarttea.org. There is still a raging debate on whether the tea or milk goes in the cup first.

Point 7: Interaction

A good project management methodology builds in interaction among team members as well as the user community.

One of the most stressful environments is the Intensive Care Unit (ICU) at any hospital. Doctors are well known for their lack of communication and terse interaction. Early in his career Dr. Dinis Miranda was instrumental in organizing the ICU at his hospital in the Netherlands. He then studied the effect of project management techniques in ICUs.

The European Union triggered the study because hospital management and government authorities were questioning the value of the ICUs. They wanted to reduce the cost of the ICUs and in some cases eliminate the functions altogether.

Over a nine-year period, Dr. Miranda and his team looked at 200 hospitals, 80,000 patients, 5,000 nurses, and 2,000 doctors throughout Europe. They introduced project management techniques into half of the hospitals and monitored them as the control group. They then compiled the results of each group and compared them.

They looked at all the tasks that are done within an ICU and gave them definitions. They assigned these tasks to the appropriate person. That way everyone knew what his or her job was and how to do it. If tasks overlapped, they set up standard protocols to resolve the overlap. For example, when should a nurse call the presiding doctor or another doctor within the hospital?

Besides the above functions, they introduced three basic collaboration processes. First, every hour a nurse visited the patient and wrote down, on a special form, all the patient's vital signs, such as blood pressure, etc. As part of this process the nurse assessed the patient's pain. Second, if possible, the nurse met with the family and talked to them about the patient's progress. Third, every day the nurse had a formal, structured meeting with the doctor or doctors to go over the reports and the outcome of the family meeting.

Miranda's team saw several positive developments just by introducing the collaborative process to the nurses and doctors. First, they saw increases in overall efficiency. Second, they observed a decrease in cost within the ICUs. Third, while the days of hospitalization increased because the patients were living longer, the overall mortality rate decreased. The result was better care and more satisfied patients (users).

Point 8: PMO

The Project Management Office (PMO) is a concept that is rapidly gaining favor as a way to align business and technical goals, and increase the odds of successful project execution in many organizations of all sizes.

The PMO is the ultimate in formal methodology. However, only about 10 percent of companies have a PMO-like organization today. Standish Group found the PMO in use in companies of various sizes, from midsize businesses to multibillion-dollar, multi-business unit corporations. A PMO is a dedicated section of the organization (one or more persons) that focuses on various aspects of project management and/or methodology. The duties of a PMO vary and often grow with the maturity of the organization. Some PMOs have one person who focuses on project scheduling or methodology, while other PMOs serve as a center of excellence for good project management practices. There are also PMOs that have large staffs and those that are deeply involved in all phases of the project, from planning through deployment. In some cases, project managers are part of the PMO and are leased out for each project.

The most common role of the PMO, as it is being applied, seems to be in the area of process monitoring, architecture, and methods control. The best practice and portfolio evaluation is performed by some of the more mature organizations. The reason most CHAOS University participants started their PMO was to gain better control over their processes and project outcomes. They had experienced failed or challenged projects that were late, over budget, or did not meet the business needs. Some Standish Group survey respondents started their PMOs in response to the need to complete high-visibility projects, such as the introduction of new technology. PMOs are also used to ensure that companies don't throw too many balls in the air at once. Too many bet the farm that projects can happen where organizational departments are in silos and overlap and duplicate requirements.

PMOs are good mechanisms for improving communications throughout the organization and getting the whole organization to pull in one direction. Even in those organizations where PMOs serve just an advisory role, most exercise a high level of influence and can make recommendations to upper management that might result in a runaway project being stopped or reorganized.

Point 9: Peer Reviews

Only a friend will tell you if you have something green stuck in your teeth. A peer review process is an important element of a formal methodology.

The Office of Government Commerce (OGC) was established in 2001 to improve procurement and project success within the British central government. A keystone program within the OGC is the Gateway Process. A key part of the gateway process is peer reviews. The OGC's Gateway Review Process has six gates. Gateway Review 0 is the strategic assessment of the project. Simply put, will the users and stakeholders support the project? At this gate, a peer reviewer might ask you such questions as: Is the business strategy robust? Does it reflect the current business conditions? Are the skills available? Is there a commitment of key roles and responsibilities? Is there an understanding of the business need? Is there an understanding of the scope of the project?

Gateway Review 1 is the business justification of the project. At this gate, a peer reviews the business need and project cost estimates, along with the potential for success. Here are a few of the questions that peers might ask you: Have all the likely stakeholders been identified? Can these critical success factors be quantified? Is there an overall project management process? Have the risks been assessed?

Gateway Review 2 is the procurement strategy of the project. Peers might ask you: Have the factors that influenced the procurement strategy been addressed? Is there adequate knowledge of existing and potential suppliers?

Gateway Review 3 is the investment decision phase of the project. This gate confirms that the recommended investment decision is appropriate before the contract is placed with a supplier or partner. Peers might ask you: Will the proposed bid deliver the business needs? Has the proposed solution affected the business strategy?

Gateway Review 4 is the readiness-for-service phase of the project. This gate looks at how ready the organization is to implement the business changes that occur before and after delivery. Peers might ask you: Does the project still meet the needs and objectives of the business and users?

Gateway Review 5 is the benefits evaluation phase of the project. This gate focuses on ensuring that the project delivers the benefits and value for the money identified in the business case and benefits plan. Peers might ask you: Is the service operating to defined parameters? The OGC Gating System is very similar to The Standish Group's gating system, but it has an extra gate for procurement and a few other items needed for a more formal government process.

Point 10: Elastic

Having a flexible formal process can improve the success rate.

Project initiatives that are rigid run the greatest risk of dissolution. This mainly refers to the rigidity of the executive team. Projects are innately perilous. There is traditionally a chain of command for mapping procedures and execution strategies. Having no formal plan of attack puts the chances of success in jeopardy. What is even more dangerous is to have a plan that has details and objectives that have not been clearly articulated to everyone involved. Time and again, lack of communication has proven to be the most damaging aspect of project failure—though it is the most preventable. The quality of work depends on the performance of the people. Project executives must be both technologically and tactically savvy to control organizational issues and meet IT goals. This requires a great deal of flexibility and resourcefulness.

The use of the formalized process and the advent of the PMO, in and of itself, cannot really control an individual project's outcome. On the down side, formality can be used improperly and when it is, that can add time and effort to the process, resulting in what is called "paralysis through analysis." On the positive side, when coupled with appropriate education and experience, a flexible formal process can improve the success rate.

There is no tool, template, or guidebook that can replace the human aspect of a project. A fool with a tool is still a fool. Project management is a team effort and requires a consensual mode of adaptable thought, especially from the project team heads. Persistent interaction with the people and the processes involved in the project is as important as, if not more so, than the tool or process.

The Web has emerged as the premiere project management resource. As a result, administering projects virtually allows variability in the project efforts amidst global expansion and a geographically distributed workforce. A flexible formal process can help you understand that the mercurial nature of projects is the bottom line. However, it will be your ability to successfully adapt to an ever-changing environment that sets you apart. Your ability to quickly recognize and respond comes from using established project management protocols that are adaptable.

In Conclusion

For Wachovia Corp., Winston-Salem, N.C., the goal of the ConnectionPlus project was to allow Internet access to its global cash management product. This was a very large project and, until Wayne Caya of Wachovia took it over, it was not going well. In 12 months Caya implemented a new formal methodology, which cut overruns and reduced errors. He used rapid, small incremental deliverables with high-quality metrics to improve the development methods. Each project was done in 90-day cycles. Since there were three groups, Wachovia released a project every month.

Establishing a formal methodology worked for Wachovia, and it can work for you too. This lesson on a formal methodology first looked at formal versus informal project methodology. The first point stated that a formal methodology must have a problem statement, requirements document, and project plan. The next three points covered these items. Point 2 covered what should be contained within a problem statement. Point 3 looked at the formal process of gathering and maintaining requirements. Point 4 considered what should be in a detailed plan. Point 5 discussed how a missed small detail can cause big problems — the "Butterfly Effect" — that could lead to project failure.

Point 6 considered the use of analogies in improving communication between users and developers. Point 7 looked at maintaining a formal methodology to support interaction between stakeholders. The case study showed how a formal methodology improved the results in hospital intensive care units. Point 8 described the Project Management Office (PMO). Point 9 discussed integrating peer reviews into your formal process. The case study looked at the British central government's OGC Gateway Process. And Point 10 suggested that having a flexible formal process can improve the success rate.

A formal methodology that is used for all IT projects across the organization can provide an understanding of the processes, methods, practices, and techniques. It can link your strategy to your technology decisions and is instrumental to maintaining an organized development environment throughout the duration of a project. Business takes place in a relationship. A formal methodology keeps stakeholders informed. It helps to eliminate inconsistency and misinformation that can promote uncertainty, which can lead to failure.

Lesson Ten: Battle of Crécy

King Phillip VI of France met King Edward III of England at the Battle of Crécy on August 26, 1346. King Phillip had 36,000 troops while King Edward was outnumbered 3-to-1 with 12,000 men. It seemed that Phillip had a major advantage over Edward. Philip's men numbered 30,000, of which 20,000 were fully outfitted mounted men-at-arms. Edward had only 5,000 men-at-arms and other infantry. The majority of Edward's troops were longbow men, while the French artillery consisted of crossbow men. Until the Battle of Crécy, bowmen were considered defensive, since the enemy had to march into their line of fire.

The crossbow was considered a superior weapon to the longbow. Its aim was more accurate and its projectiles flew faster and farther. However, the average crossbow man could only shoot, at best, four arrows a minute while the average longbow man could shoot 24 arrows a minute. The battle started with the crossbow men advancing 150 yards of the English's frontline. The 7,000 English longbow men fired with such precision and efficiency that they killed the majority of the crossbow men in less than one minute.

The remainder retreated right into the French men-at-arms. The French soldiers, thinking that the crossbow men were the English, trampled them with their horses. Men and horses began piling up and the English longbow men continued to volley. The French charged another 15 times. Each time the English longbow men picked them off like flies. At the end of the battle, 10,000 French soldiers lay dead, while only 100 Englishmen were killed. The English won the day using the right tool.

Tools that help you to collaborate with all project contributors and stakeholders are the most useful. They can point out weaknesses and tension points, determine priority, as well as identify potential setbacks before they become insurmountable. They can give you the power to communicate.

Point 1: Toolkit

If clothes make the man (or woman), tools and infrastructure make the project.

Requirement tools, for example, seem to have the largest influence on the success of a project. These tools, if used as a platform for communications among all the stakeholders such as executive sponsors and users, can provide a huge advantage. You need to consider this kind of tool as essential to the project.

Standish Group has found that successful projects have a slightly higher use of design/analysis tools than those projects that do not utilize such tools. However, the data showing that these products actually do help with the success rate is inconclusive. Standish Group research has also found that projects that use a modeling tool have a higher rate of failure than those did that do not use one. However, it should be noted that modeling tools are used in larger projects and larger projects also have a greater failure rate. Like the design/analysis tool, this tool should not be selected just to improve success rates.

Project management tools are primarily used by the project manager and typically offer tracking, planning, and scheduling. Traditionally, project management tools have helped when collected information is accurate and shared. Far too often, however, this is not the case and project management tools are used simply to justify poor results. Since practically every firm uses some sort of project management tool, the overall research results do not reflect their benefit. In fact, failed projects have a higher use of project management tools than successful projects. Project management tools must be actively used and require constant adjustments to ensure success.

It is clear from Standish Group's latest research that components deployed within a standard infrastructure along with easy-to-use management tools can have a major positive impact on the outcome of a project. As components can be plugged, played, and deleted more easily from the infrastructure, technology is evolving to ensure interoperability between these movable structures. Object and component technology represents transparent, interactive exchange among disparate programs and platforms.

Point 2: Vocabulary

A common and agreed upon vocabulary should be part of every toolkit.

During one of Standish Group's CHAOS University sessions, the class broke up into six workshop "focus groups" to undertake a variety of topics, one of which was titled "Infrastructure Management." In this workshop we undertook to delve into the requirements for managing infrastructure and the accompanying problems and issues.

Not wanting to steer the groups in any way, we first instructed them to define the term "Infrastructure Management." To do so, the groups had to discuss what was meant by the word "infrastructure." It's a word that gets thrown around quite frequently in our industry and one that we discovered is quite versatile. Some attendees focused on "software infrastructure," others on "hardware infrastructure." There were debates over whether humans were part of the equation. What about electricity and air conditioning? Is the phone system included? What about the concrete of which the basement of the building are made? Surely these things are considered infrastructure — or are they?

Having a versatile word can be a good thing. After all, minimizing the number of terms and words in our industry is helpful. However, it can also be bad. Many of our workgroups started debating the management issue right away, only to later discover the source of many arguments had to do with confusion over what exactly they were trying to manage.

A dictionary is good place to start. For example, Webster's Dictionary defines infrastructure as the underlying foundation or basic framework of a system or organization. I'll leave it up to you to decide what that includes and excludes, but make sure that your fellow stakeholders share your perception. It probably isn't as important what is in or out, but rather that you all agree on what is in or out. If someone assumes you are going to build something, and you and that individual don't understand the basic vocabulary, you already are in deep trouble.

One of the main issues that led to Standish Group's CHAOS research is poor communication. We have spent many hours discussing how vital it is to use a standard vocabulary that is understood by all parties involved in the project.

Point 3: Requirements

A requirements management tool needs to be at the top of the shopping list for any firm involved in developing software applications.

Standish Group research shows that the use of requirements management tools has the biggest impact on the success of a project. These tools, if used as a platform for communications among the stakeholders, can provide enormous benefit. A requirements management tool can be used as a way for you to convey to the stakeholders that you understand the business problem.

Losing sight of requirements is often the first step on the path to challenged projects that do not meet specifications, or end up being canceled. Requirements management tools complement and automate a sound process, such as an agile method. It's important to note that a requirements management tool is not a substitute for a nonexistent requirements management process; the tool supports the process. The need to manage project requirements is inescapable. Requirements are the building blocks of all actions and projects. A requirement equates to a need, where a need to eat precipitates a visit to a restaurant or grocery store, or a need for a feature/function drives a software development project.

The climate is ripe for acceptance of requirements management tools in the ever-changing, complex world of software development. Available tools range from those catering to complex engineering requirements to those geared toward less technical, but equally important, business requirements. No tool will succeed without a corresponding requirements management process, which must exist first. Requirements tools were originally developed for the military aerospace industry, but are now commonly used for all commercial enterprises large and small.

Standish Group recommends selecting a tool based on your organization's specific needs and environment. Buying more or less tool than you need and can effectively use is not only economically impractical, but can contribute to a lack of tool acceptance due to too much or too little function. A tool that doesn't fit an organization's needs will quickly become shelfware. Choosing the right tool to complement an existing requirements management process is a step on the road to project success.

Point 4: Changes

Project changes are inevitable, but change management tools can help you keep change under control.

When you start a software development project, one thing you can be sure of is that the code is going to change and change and change again. User feedback, new or altered features, and bugs all trigger updates. If the software hits its target there will be fresh changes for new versions. In active software and mission-critical applications, changes are a never-ending cycle.

Even for perfect code, managing all the pieces is a daunting and difficult task. Before approving a new build, you have to be sure that all the parts are finished, tested, and work together. When something goes wrong, you have to revert to a previous version and the chore is to get the backup inventory and environment requirements just right.

"Change management software can drive the whole process," said Darcy Wiborg-Weber, vice president of product development for Telelogic, a global provider of solutions for automating and supporting best practices across the enterprise. "It supports the entire software development life cycle, from product development through testing, release, and maintenance."

A Web-based change management system can be used or viewed by managers, developers, testers, stakeholders, and anyone else who needs access to project information. Stakeholders can submit requests and review progress. Managers can assign tasks or view who is working on what areas of the project. You can also generate progress reports from a change management system.

Coordinating development and maintenance tasks for a big project is a monumental job. Today, with an increasing number of projects carried out across distributed locations, sometimes in different countries, it's a challenge to keep track of ongoing activities, code, versions, and builds without ending up with gray hair or a nervous breakdown. The heart of the change management system is like a software asset repository. This repository has information about projects, tasks, personnel, and processes.

All of this accounts for the increasing popularity of change management products. A good change management package provides an orderly framework for tracking the progress of a diverse group of developers, testers, and maintainers, and controlling the resulting software throughout its life cycle.

Point 5: WebEx

WebEx, a Web-based collaboration product, is a great tool for managing projects.

WebEx can provide communication, demonstration, education, and support services no matter where you are in the world. To the meeting participant, the WebEx interface appears as a simple, easy-to-use menu of meeting options. From conference calls to presentations and sharing applications, a host of different information-sharing capabilities are available and easy to access. However, underneath these simple screens lies a Web-based, real-time communications infrastructure. WebEx technology is based on the company's global and interactive communications infrastructure. The interactive system includes three basic components: the interactive network, the interactive platform, and the interactive services

Face-to-face project meetings and product demonstrations are expensive, inconvenient, and difficult to coordinate. This problem is not going away as society and the industry continue to fragment and become increasingly scattered geographically. WebEx service is as natural as picking up the phone. Using WebEx for collaboration management has a threefold benefit: It provides a virtual open channel of communication that gives everyone a voice; project details are distributed effectively; and activities are self-coordinated, expedited, and documented.

I have been working with WebEx since its inception. Standish Group was actually the very first user. WebEx worked with us to help us provide better services to our clients. These services include presenting research to single and multiple clients in a more timely fashion; providing feedback on user and vendor presentations; performing complex data acquisition, such as cost of ownership data; and conducting concept and focus group testing. In all these cases, WebEx technology increased the speed of delivery, improved the level of service, and reduced expenses. At Standish Group, we feel strongly that the technology can improve project success. Every month we present our new research through what we call Research Exchanges, or REXs.

More than a quarter of businesses have successfully used collaboration services such as WebEx to help with their collaboration project management activities. We stress that using WebEx for collaboration management resources and techniques cannot guarantee success because project management, by nature, is a hazardous venture. However, WebEx can certainly improve communication—a significant foothold to reach success.

Point 6: Reasoning

Automated software testing tools help keep the bugs out.

According to Standish Group's Comparative Economic Normalization Technology Study (CENTS), which tracks downtime of 2,000 mission-critical applications on a monthly basis, software bugs (or software quality) are the leading causes of downtime. In fact, they account for almost half of all instances of downtime. In financial terms, they account for 55 percent of all downtime costs, causing monetary losses of almost $300 billion annually.

Software bugs are far more prevalent than hardware errors. In fact, software failures account for more costs than hardware failures by a ratio of almost a 3-to-1. It is also true that software bugs account for far more downtime than hardware failures.

Yet many companies spend a great deal of money and time on hardware quality, but spend little time and money to ensure software quality. Even for those companies that do devote considerable resources to inspect their code, the effort is so complex that errors are still inevitable. That said quality hardware is relatively easy to implement, whereas quality software is hard to implement. In fact, companies that do not spend the time and money up front to correct bugs end up paying for it in downtime and corrective efforts after the code is released. There is a better way.

Standish Group conducted a series of interviews with companies to find out how much they spend on manual code inspection and testing, and whether inspection tools or services are efficient and cost-effective. Consider the impact on one commercial software developer. Prior to investing in automated inspection tools, this company relied solely on a manual testing and inspection process. Before releasing code to its customers, the company would assemble a team of code inspectors to perform spot checks throughout the code. It would take many weeks and still the code would have many critical bugs. Implementing an automated inspection process enabled the company to perform the procedure in half the time and with a quarter of the bugs, meaning they eliminated three-quarters of the bugs.

While automated testing and inspection will not eliminate all errors, users generally agree that the process reduces them. More importantly, automated testing and inspection solutions can reduce the overall project time and once again, time is the enemy of all projects.

Point 7: Sprint

A standardized software infrastructure can be a powerful tool for project teams.

Sprint's experience is a good example. In 1999 Sprint was the only telecommunications provider that had an active presence in local, long distance, national cellular, and PCS (personal communications service) markets. It had a complete fiber-optic long-distance network and was one of the largest carriers of Internet traffic. Sprint's customer satisfaction and revenue were among the best in the telecom industry. However, the telecom market is one of the most competitive and Sprint could not afford to stand still. The issue was, most of its business systems consisted of stovepipe applications with an alphabet soup of products, which included IBM mainframes running CICS, UNIX servers running Oracle, HP NonStop Servers running its own proprietary products, and Wintel servers. This type of infrastructure was keeping Sprint from developing new products and services rapidly.

Sprint wanted to build a standard software infrastructure to increase efficiency and flexibility, build more complex business rules, and be able to launch new products and market programs more quickly. The infrastructure needed to be conducive to the assimilation of new technologies while embracing legacy systems in a seamless manner. The new infrastructure would be based on a message delivery system that could evolve independently and also allow independent evolution on the applications and technical architectures. Sprint had been building large-scale-distributed applications since the late '80s and moved to an object technology base in 1993.

In March 1998 Sprint set out to build a common software infrastructure based on object technology and a message middleware system. One year later Sprint had the ability to reduce programming by creating a software environment that was both highly available and scalable. This enabled developers to focus on the applications and isolate changes in the environment. Sprint's software infrastructure also provided for fine-grained error reporting, which enabled rapid problem determination and correction.

From a project and program management perspective, Sprint's software infrastructure helps identify and mitigate risks early on by allowing the development staff to focus on the application issues rather than the environmental issues of the application. Designs and requirements documents require minimum platform considerations. Since it is a standard infrastructure, the learning curve was reduced to a minimal set of installed products. The common infrastructure also appealed to workers and therefore helped Sprint in the recruiting and retaining of staff.

Point 8: Vendors

Try to find trustworthy vendors.

Remember the old adage, "You can tell a vendor is lying when his lips are moving." It is a funny and cute way of pointing out a serious problem: How can companies determine when a vendor is lying, and what can they do to protect themselves?

At a CHAOS University session, we asked participants to provide us with "the rest of the story" and how they can tell if a vendor is lying. The group said one sure sign a vendor may be lying is when the vendor offers a lot of small talk and postpones getting down to the heart of the matter. Or, participants said to be on alert when a vendor comes into the initial meeting with the words, "What can we do for you?" when, in fact, the vendor initiated the sales call. Another sign is when a vendor promises that it has the right solution, but hasn't even asked what the problems are.

Participants also warned to look out for vendors who bring in an army of sales and technical people when there are only one or two people on the client side. This brings an unbalanced nature to the meeting and makes for some awkward and perhaps uncomfortable gatherings. Other signs of untruthfulness include avoiding eye contact, evading questions or offering long and involved answers to simple questions, and finally, passing the buck. In a recent virtual focus group one participant said his projects were being killed by a thousand cuts from vendors delivering infrastructure software with minor bugs in the code. Pretty soon he was two months behind on many of his projects.

We also wanted to know how the participants handled vendor relationships. We first asked them, "What can you do when you think a vendor is lying to you?" Our last question asked how participants could make sure a vendor would deliver the goods it promised. The solutions the participants came up with were: first, you should get a list of the last three clients they have worked with, not the best three. Second, be sure to ask for references for projects that were not delivered on time and on budget. Third, ask the references about the quality of code and how the vendor handed the situation.

Point 9: Open Source

Don't reinvent the wheel.

Standish Group research indicates that open source objects are currently fulfilling about 10 percent of the features and requirements for custom software. Standish Group thinks this number will grow as organizations learn that major systems can be deployed faster and cheaper without the burden of larger and complex packages. In that regard, you should be able to reduce your organization's software expenditures by more than 25 percent by using open source products and objects.

The process is fairly simple. The following example shows how Standish Group created a major asset management application with two people in less than six months. If we did it from scratch, writing all the code ourselves, it would have taken 20 person-years. My experience indicates if the government did it, it would have taken 200 person-years.

We first went to SourceForge.net and looked at a number of applications that seemed promising. We decided to download the two closest to our needs. We then tested and reviewed the code, and played with both applications. We picked the one that seemed to be written the best and was close to the technology we were currently using. We then pruned (refactored) the code by taking out all the features and functions we did not need or want. This amounted to more than 60 percent of the code. We broke it, then we fixed it. This task took us about 60 person-days to complete. This was our baseline.

We then looked at our bare minimum requirements. Since we have a standard infrastructure in place, our developers did not need to be concerned about this issue. The requirements document only needed to be concerned with the business rules and features. A standard infrastructure also cuts down on integration requirements, which in some cases can be the major part of the task. The developers then built the application based on these minimum requirements. This took two months, with several users' observations. We then tested the application using automatic testing and inspection tools, in addition to manual testing. From here we deployed the application on our Web servers as part of our VirtualADVISOR suite. Here is where the Web is the right tool for this job. Since we have a no-release policy, we update, add features, and maintain the application on-the-fly.

Chart 16

How do you calculate ROI for individual requirements?

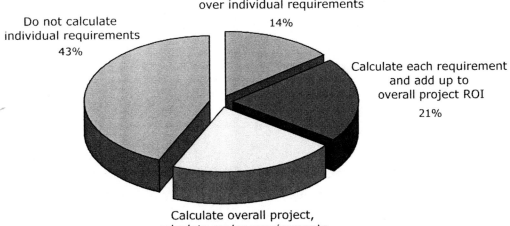

Calculate overall project and allocate
over individual requirements
14%

Do not calculate
individual requirements
43%

Calculate each requirement
and add up to
overall project ROI
21%

Calculate overall project,
calculate major requirements
and allocate the rest
21%

Source: DARTS March 2006

Point 10: Optimizing

By understanding the ROI of each feature and function, scope can be changed by priorities for the maximum return.

Standish Group research has found that the higher the number of features and functions that get built, the less they are used. The average is 17 percent of features built. For example, if an organization were to build 100 percent of the functions users wanted, only 11 percent would be used. On the other hand, if an organization were to build 25 percent of the features and functions specified, then we estimate the average would move up to 26 percent. In other words if you had 100 features and did them all, the users would only use 11 of them. However if you did the most important 25 they would use 8. You would only be missing 3 features. You would build 75 features to get 3. These features could be built in a later version. Therefore, there has to be a new approach to looking at requirements since all features and functions will have their own ROI. Some functions may have no return at all, so why develop them?

This process for examining ROI for feature/function is iterative and dynamic. First, start with an ROI for the project; remember a reliable estimate is a key ingredient to an accurate ROI. Then, calculate an ROI on each of the "features and functions" and add them up. You need to make sure that the individual ROI matches the overall ROI. Now, do the same for the risk.

The Standish Group assessment system and optimizer consists of an experience database and a wisdom engine. The experience database, or CHAOS Database, contains 115 project attributes with more than 50,000 cases accrued to date. The wisdom engine is used to calculate the cost, risk, and gain. For every project and requirement, cost, risk, and gain inputs are submitted to the Genomic Optimizer. Standish Group's Genomic Optimizer has special algorithms and processes, similar to DNA analysis, and calculates the best possible combinations to give you the maximum value.

Standish Group provides four critical building blocks to calculate cost, risk, and gain. First, experience field operatives, known as the STARs, work with you for the first inputs. Second, in-house specialists who have decades of experience in estimating cost, risk, and gain verify the inputs and provide vital advice. Third, the specialists also use sophisticated estimating utilities. Fourth is the CHAOS database of 50,000 projects. These four elements provide a comprehensive estimating process that has never before been available in the IT community.

In Conclusion

In general, tools that can shorten a project and help teams focus on the important items go a long way toward helping to achieve success. Having a toolkit with requirements, change, and collaboration management should help you along the way. Using open source objects and other methods to shortcut development is another way to increase success rates.

This lesson on tools and infrastructure started with a look at a project toolkit. Point 1 considered the types of tools you need to manage and control your projects. Point 2 discussed use of a standard vocabulary to facilitate proper communications as part of your toolkit. Point 3 covered requirements management tools. Standish Group research clearly shows that requirements management tools have a huge impact on the success of a project. Point 4 considered the benefits of change management software in the dynamic world of developing application software. Point 5 looked at WebEx as a collaboration management tool, especially useful for distributed and geographically dispersed teams.

Point 6 focused on using inspection and testing tools like you would use spell check on documents, since application software bugs are the leading cause of downtime. Point 7 reflected on the benefits of a standard infrastructure through the eyes of Sprint. Point 8 looked at how to recognize trustworthy and untrustworthy vendors. Point 9 considered the benefits of using open source software and components to jump-start a project and provide the baseline. The case study highlighted how Standish Group created a major software product using this technique. The last point talked about optimizing your project portfolio and your requirements set by looking at cost, risk, and gain as the central factors.

While tools can be beneficial, remember that the use of tools for tools' sake may actually be more hurtful than helpful. If the tool is used only after the fact to document history, it is useless. If data is collected on the project and programs are not near-real-time, then it is too late. Project management tools should be used in ways that foster and promote communication and collaboration.

Summary

The Federal Bureau of Investigation (FBI) has invested millions of taxpayer dollars in project management training, skills, and technology to prepare itself for resolving projects successfully. Yet in March 2005, the FBI canceled the Virtual Case File project after spending $170 million of those taxpayer dollars. This was a very important project, which would allow the agency to share information with other law enforcement and intelligence agencies. The FBI is not alone — this is just one of more than 100,000 projects that will be cancelled throughout the world this year. Martin Cobb of the Treasury Board of Canada Secretariat said in 1995, "We know why projects fail, we know how to prevent their failure — so why do they still fail?" This later became known as Cobb's Paradox. Therefore, we have to consider Cobb's Paradox: "So why do they still fail?"

The first lesson in this book, "Guadalcanal," covered user involvement. As stated, user involvement is the number one CHAOS Success Factor. It has been some time since lack of user involvement has been the leading cause of project failure. This is because most organizations now recognize the need to involve the user and build applications that they will utilize. However, user involvement still belongs in the number one position because ignoring it remains the most deadly error. It is almost certain that without user involvement, a project is doomed to fail. In example after example, we see that a healthy relationship between the users and developers keeps everyone on track to a successful project resolution. This does not mean simply giving the users what they want; it is making certain they get what they need.

Lesson Two, "Remember the Alamo," focused on executive management support. A project needs to begin and end with the vision of the prime executive. Projects that lack a steadfast commitment and a clear perception of business goals have a very difficult time achieving a successful resolution. Many of today's executives are impatient and become frustrated, causing them to drop support for long-running projects. Early deliverables, demonstrable progress, and swift financial benefits are essential in modern application life cycles to maintain that vital executive support and interest.

The third lesson, "Vietnam," talked about clear business objectives. While this factor seems obvious, time and time again we see various stakeholders who have different project goals. A concise and comprehensive vision statement that is agreed upon, or at least acknowledged by the stakeholders, will go a long way toward ensuring a successful project resolution. This vision should be tested from time to time to make sure that the stakeholders have the correct perception of the project goals. As the project runs it course, this vision may vary and must be updated to reflect any changes in direction; these changes must be communicated to the team. One way to do this is to have a peer review at each major stage and delivery point. Another way is to institute a formal collaboration procedure to make sure everyone is on the same page.

Lesson Four, "The Great Molasses Flood," concentrated on optimizing scope. Doing too much for too little is one of the leading causes of project failure. The first step in optimizing scope and requirements is to know why a project needs to be done and to match its requirements with a business case. This can be accomplished by providing a straightforward definition for each major requirement. It should be noted that Standish Group has found that the majority of features built are never used. One method to avoid overbuild is to first prioritize each feature and then do a cost/benefit/risk analysis on each of the major features.

Lesson Five, "Cotton Gin," considered the agile process. If there ever was a silver bullet to kill the demons of project failure, it is an iterative and agile process. In one iterative and agile methodology, developers work in pairs and test scripts are written before the code. In The Standish Group methodology there are no milestones, and requirements are time-boxed and delivered in stepping-stones. A stepping-stone is different from a milestone because it is an actual deliverable. The process starts with focusing on implementing the bare minimum requirements, called the "baseline." Software is then added to the baseline in small increments and delivered on an ongoing basis. There are no software releases; the system is built over a standard infrastructure that allows for constant deliverables, updates, and fixes.

Lesson Six, "George Washington," covered project management expertise. The right project manager with the right process can sometimes save even the most doomed project. Standish Group research has shown that projects are likely to be less challenged and more successful when there is a proficient project management process in place. Proficiency starts with project management fundamentals and leadership skills. Expertise in project management includes the ability to communicate with users and executives, good judgment, and general business skills. In this regard, the lesson considered obtaining and maintaining connections and how important they are to the success of a project. A Project Management Office (PMO) can be used to provide a central repository for this expertise and knowledge.

Lesson Seven, "Diogenes the Cynic," centered on investment a nd financial management. Project plans need to look more like business plans, for they truly are business plans. A business plan will always have a section with detailed expenditures. In a project plan, the detailed expenses are the cost of each requirement. These costs then can be rolled up into a project estimate. This estimate can be benchmarked against projects of similar size within and outside the organization. A peer review can resolve differences. The project plan must be a living document that is constantly updated as changes are introduced. A gating system would be a great asset in managing a project's finances. A gating system defines a series of processes and peer reviews to be performed at each major project event.

In Lesson Eight, "New Model Army," the focus was on skilled resources. The New England Patriots won their third Super Bowl in four years based on three key elements: talented players in each position, a cohesive team, and proficient coaches. Successful projects have the same elements: competent developers, stakeholders who work as a team, and management that communicates strategy and goals. These assets, coupled with standards, performance measurements, best practices, and incentives, make a successful resolution achievable. It is doubtful that a project could be successful without these elements. Sufficient training programs and staff augmentations can sometimes fill in the gaps for various deficiencies.

Lesson Nine, "War Room," looked at formal methodology. It all starts with a problem statement and a plan to solve a business problem. After that, organizations need to assess how formal a methodology they need. At the minimum, a methodology needs to track progress and perform cost accounting. As noted earlier, a gating system can greatly reduce waste and increase financial rewards. Standish Group research has shown that large organizations with PMOs have a slightly better track record than those without such an organization. We also think there should be a formal process to analyze each requirement or feature for cost, benefit, and risk.

The last lesson, "Battle of Crécy," deliberated the benefits of tools and infrastructure. Tools by themselves do not promote success; the proper use of the tools does. Project management tools and suites have a poor track record of actual use, but those project managers who use them correctly have improved their likelihood of project success. Web-based collaboration services, such as WebEx, offer a way to communicate with stakeholders quickly and easily, even for complicated events such as demonstrating prototypes. Organizations with IT operations on the same level or higher than IT development have a much better track record in the deployment part of the project than those that do not have equal partners.

Certainly the big three pillars of project success are user involvement, executive support, and clear business objectives. Organizations that ignore these realities run the risk of poor project resolutions. On Standish Group's point scale, these factors account for 50 percent of the points. Therefore, by just focusing on these success factors you can reduce your risk of failure by as much as 50 percent. These factors also are the simplest to implement, assess, and test. If that is the case, then again we ask, "So why do they still fail?"

The answer to this perplexing paradox may lie in the five deadly sins of project management—ambition, arrogance, ignorance, fraudulence, and abstinence. They are always present in some form, but any one of them taken to the extreme can void all the good work of the big three, and in combination the five deadly sins are truly deadly.

Ambition, or in actuality over-ambition, can take many forms; for example, trying to build something too fast with too many people that is designed to be all things to all users. Arrogance can take the form of a prime executive who overrides user input and forces implementation of his or her mistaken perception of how things should work. We just recently saw this happen in a project and the organization had to write-off several million dollars. A good test for ignorance is if the requirements document states that the new system must "do everything that the old system did." If that's truly the goal, then why develop a new system? This is not a requirement, but a death sentence. Fraudulence may perhaps be a little strong, but we have too often seen people underestimate costs in order to get the go-ahead to start a project. And finally, abstinence is when key people do not participant in the project.

The other seven success factors are the "seven dwarfs" of project management — scope optimization, agile processes, project management expertise, financial management, skilled resources, formal methodology, and tools. They are like supporting actors in a good movie. Without them the movie would not work. They can and do mitigate the effects of the five deadly sins. For example, an agile process can warn the prime executive that the project is failing early enough to put the project back on the right track.

Optimizing scope and requirements can get rid of broad proclamations such as, "The new system must do everything the old system does." Financial management can expose poor estimating.

The original Standish Group CHAOS report in 1994 discussed a paper written by Alfred Spector, then president of Transarc Corporation, comparing bridge building to software development. The premise of his 1986 paper was that bridges are normally built on time and on budget, and they do not fall down. In comparison, software development projects at the time never came in on time or on budget and always broke.

The industry has come a long way since then. There are now many techniques, processes, and tools that can help you build application software, and success rates have improved. A few years ago on a tour of the Sydney Opera House, the guide portrayed its construction as a great feat over much adversity. Of course this is very true, but most of this adversity was self-inflected by poor project management techniques and processes.

Projects are risky and when pushing the envelope like the Sydney Opera House you do not need to make it harder on yourself. Just remember; communication, collaboration, and simplicity are keys to successful projects. Money is the root of all evil, and time is the enemy of all projects. Bringing projects to a successful resolution is not easy. It takes hard work, dedication to the success factors, and sometimes a little luck.

W

Wachovia, 141
WebEx, 15, 20, 75, 76, 80, 148, 155, 160
WIIFM, 24, 53
Wright, Judy, 34

Y

Yardstick, 51
Yield, 67

HERE'S WHAT YOU'LL GET:

ACCESS TO THE CHAOS KNOWLEDGE CENTER

Here you will find the complete published works from the CHAOS research effort including charts, classic reports like the CHAOS Chronicles 3.0, cases studies, and talks. Our Dynamic CHAOS Chronicles, which is updated on continuous basis, also gives you the ability to create your own personalized CHAOS Chronicles.

MONTHLY CHAOS ACTIVITY NEWSLETTER

CHAOS University Newsletter is a four-page bulletin that is sent out once a month. It covers news, data, and events around PM issues and related topics

AND MUCH MORE!

A one year subscription gives you access to the freshest research available on project management success – gleaned from our many years of studying project failures.

REAL CASES – REAL DATA
TO HELP YOUR PROJECTS BE SUCCESSFUL!

To join, go to: http://www.standishgroup.com/

CHAOS University Outreach Programs are a one-day staff development and education workshop modeled after the CHAOS University multi-day retreat offered by Standish Group since 1995. These courses are intended for staff involved in project management at the manager, director, and leadership levels.

In each workshop, eight to ten participants become a peer review group brought in as "fresh eyes" to look at the current state of a project and report their findings back to the Board of Directors. During this multi-segmented, interactive workshop, which includes group discussion, presentation, and professional Standish Group moderation, the group will explore ways to identify clues that lead to solutions, take action to overcome problems, and raise the project success quotient.

For more information on CHAOS University programs go to:

http://www.standishgroup.com/events

Coming in 2007 a new book by Jim Johnson

The Public Execution of Miss Scarlet

A fictional Tale of a Project in Peril

The Standish Group International, Inc.

Our Company

We focus on failure to help you succeed. The Standish Group is based in West Yarmouth, Massachusetts and is the Information Technology leader in project and value performance. We are a group of highly dedicated professionals with years of practical experience in assessing risk, cost, return and value for Information Technology (IT) Investments.

Our Beginnings

The Standish Group was formed in 1985, with a vision. It was to collect case information on real-life IT failures and environments. Why? We do this in order to profile your projects and environments against those cases and deliver advice based on collective wisdom.

Our Mission

The Standish Group's mission is to make you more successful and help to show ways to improve your success rates and increase the value of your IT investments. We build and provide solutions that can reduce your risk and improve as well as accelerate the value of your Information Technology. The Standish Group provides IT investment planning research and services, such as, project assessments, requirements optimization, Total Cost of Ownership (TCO), Return on Investment (ROI), Risk, and Value Analysis based on years of high quality, independent primary research.

Our Customers

The Standish Group's customers embrace and focus on our solutions to help them have a better understanding of the risk and value of their technology investments. These clients encompass a range from the very largest organizations to new start-ups and are comprised of the largest banks, security firms, telecommunication companies, manufacturers, government agencies, and technology providers.

Our Values

Innovation and Understanding
Enthusiasm and Hard Work
Rigor & Quality
Respect for the Individual
Pride in the Company
Enjoyment of Life

James (Jim) H. Johnson

Mr. James (Jim) H. Johnson is the founder and chairman of The Standish Group. He has been professionally involved in the computer industry for over 30 years and has a long list of published papers, articles and speeches. He has a combination of technical, marketing, and research achievements focused on mission-critical applications and technology. He is best known for his research on project and system failures.

Jim is a pioneer of modern research techniques and continues to advance in the research industry through virtual focus groups and case-based analytical technology.